# Alice Paul, A Suffragist for Today
## *Moving Forward, Looking Back*

## Patricia Cuff

Cover SISTERHOOD IS POWERFUL Photo by Sophia Tull

Library of Congress, Prints and Photographs Division, c. 1918 BIOG File Alice Paul

Published by DPCarr Press

http://www.patriciacuff.com/

# Acknowledgements

So many thanks to so many people. Margaret Maring and Diane de Onis took time out from their summer tennis game to be my first reviewers. Fern Truitt sorted out the dates correctly. Sarah Purcell's encouragement nudged me off the starting line. My loyal supporter and fellow environmentalist Beckie St. John, reenacts Alice Paul, while correctly attired in white, a fashionable lid perched atop. Regina Sheridan mentors from Florida.

Marybeth Gallagher and Thomas Weber enlarged my platform and stay available for technical support. Library of Congress Staffers Mary Champagne and Abby Yochelson remained in touch.

Canny advice from Patricia Donahue was always just a click away. Anne Gallagher and Savannah Cuff designed the cover. The Cuff Triplets and Casey Donahue provided a teen perspective, and gained a modern acquaintance with the suffragists.

Steely eyed, Nancy Carr edits with exquisite precision. Technical aid for ailing computers was delivered by Andy Carr. But Danielle Carr, did the heavy lifting, gracefully navigating the mechanics of book publishing in the 21st century way.

# Alice Paul, A Suffragist for Today
## *Moving Forward, Looking Back*

## Read This Before You Begin: *Why This Book is **Important***

Stop reading right now if you don't agree with this book's thesis that ***any abuse of or injustice against women is totally unacceptable***. Sexual harassment, in any form, is deplorable. Though some powerful men have been punished for their behavior lately, make no mistake, women's abuse remains a global issue even today.[1]

The **#Metoo Movement** has its origins in women's history, since there were times and places where women mobilized successfully and faced down the impossible. An example, Alice Paul, the avatar of organized resistance, was sent out by her "friends" to pass an amendment to the U.S. Constitution. The leading suffrage organization gifted her with abundant ill-will and a $10.00 budget. So she created the ***first ever* Women's March** in Washington, DC. She upended expectations to produce a spectacular display of women's determination for equality. We can learn much from Alice Paul and the amazing women who were her cohorts in the crusade for women's rights. We know that likeminded, persistent women like the #Metoo generation, determined by a single purpose, can permanently alter society also.

This book will invite you to tread new intellectual territory. In telling the story of Alice Paul's unstinting battle for women's rights, alternate opinions and tactics are laid out for your consideration. I call these issues **"Ponderables"** because in eras of intense emotion, political or otherwise, an intelligent response calls for the thoughtful examination of

---

[1] Kristof, Nicholas, WuDunn, Sheryl, *Half The Sky* (New York: Alfred A. Knopf, 2010)

opposing views. (For a crash course in viewing alternate viewpoints try YouTube "The Vinegar Tasters".)

The **Ponderable** here is concerned with the methods used to counteract the daunting reality of the oppression. Alice Paul was taught well by the English suffragettes' play book: 1. arrest, 2. jail, 3. hunger strike, 4. force feeding, 5. public clamor,6. embarrassed politicians, 7. release, 8. suffragette win. Her opposite suffragist Carrie Chapman Catt's method had to do with uncritical support of the biased President, Woodrow Wilson. His support held the power to influence the vote, so she would sweet talk him into agreement. Which method was most effective: active aggression or passive aggression… in your face or in your ear?

Check out the history books to determine which of the two woman is celebrated as responsible for the passage of the 20th amendment which gave women the vote. Furthermore, check out the space given to the whole issue of women's suffrage. **Ponderable** Who determines the content of the history books? Are history books aimed at a specific audience?

Alice Paul deliberately sought the support of wealthy socialites, particularly Alva Belmont, who contributed generously to the cause, thus affecting its outcome. This practice is well alive today where wealthy individuals contribute to their favored congressmen. But Alice also counted each rich or poor suffragist as crucial. **Ponderable** Who are more effective as legislative advocates, big donors or energized voters?

American history is replete with racism and the suffragists were not unaware of its impact on their cause. The **Ponderable** here is to question the concept that southern white supremacy should have been overlooked for the "greater good of all women." The passage of the Anthony Amendment would mean all women could vote. "All women" included northern black women. (Sadly the 19th Amendment did not interfere with the literacy tests and poll taxes which generally disenfranchised both black men and women until the Voting Rights Act of 1965.)  In the course of reading *Alice Paul, Suffragist for Today* you will encounter more **Ponderables**. Let's talk. How do you feel about money in politics, or some Suffragist's racism?  Or any other topic related to women's rights.

Moving Forward, Look Back to Alice, because never intimidated, she persisted.


Chat with me and friends at my website, Patriciacuff.com

# Contents

## Part One: Creeping to Sweeping Change
## (3900 BC-19<sup>th</sup> Century AD)

## Part Two: Metamorphosis (1906-1910)

## Part Three: Alice Evolves, Her American Journey
## January, 1910 - March, 1913

## Part Four: The Wheels Grind
## (March 4, 1913-April 6, 1917)

## Part Five: The Descent into Hell

## January 9, 1917-November 28, 1917

## Part Six: The Beginning of the End of the End of the Beginning

## December 1917 –August 24, 1918

# Alice Paul, A Suffragist for Today
## Moving Forward, Looking Back

*Tell me, what is it to you plan to do*
*With your one wild and precious life?*
Mary Oliver, *The Summer Day*

# Prologue

## Votes for Women, the Battle Cry

It's a chilly daybreak, in London, on November 9, 1909. As sunlight streaks across the sky, a line of ragged scrubwomen file past a guard and enter the Lord Mayor's seat of power, the Guildhall. The women are there to clean the hall for his cabinet members' dining that evening. The guard scrutinizes each woman. He sees nothing unusual about two of the bedraggled young workers passing by him hauling their buckets and brooms. Just another pair of faceless women…maybe.

Day long, the police search the banquet hall. They know they are targets of clever angry women and are looking for infiltrators. They scour every possible nook and cranny sticking long pins into dark corners, hoping to stab a woman secreted there. Two "scrubwomen" don't clean; they slide under benches there. All day, the two women remain painfully hidden, silent, petrified as even one guard comes so close his cape brushes the hair of the curled up woman.

Many long hours later the party begins. The two cramped women crawl out from under their benches. Amidst the hilarity and with all eyes on the mayor, they quickly slip up to a glass enclosed balcony. One, just as the Lord Mayor begins his address, whips off her shoe and smashes the balcony glass showering shards below. Their voices resound, "Votes for Women!" "Votes for Women!" It is the battle cry of oppressed women. It is the plea and the pledge of the English suffragette. And once again this irksome band of women have outfoxed the mayor!

For this caper, Alice Paul and Amelia Brown will pay a high price.

# Part One: Creeping to Sweeping Change (3900 BC-19ᵗʰ Century)

## Chapter 1
## Millennia of Abuse of Women

Actually, Alice Paul's life began centuries before she was born.

The injustice, disrespect and, often, the abuse of women which Alice confronted later, was commonplace in most ancient societies. It continued as the norm through the largest part of history. Aristotle, the Greek genius, though he knew a lot about physics, was dead wrong about women. He taught that man is by nature superior to the female and so the man should rule and the woman should be ruled. Later, the more accepting first century AD Roman Empire, which placed great value on the home and family, enhanced a woman's role, a break in oppression. That ended soon.

Things went back to "normal" during the Middle Ages, the fifth to the fifteenth centuries. Then only men mattered and women were considered soulless people. Rich women might be a little less soulless, but they still had to obey men and couldn't marry without Dad's permission and she'd better have a son or keep trying. Joan of Arc was an exception. She obeyed her inner voices and led the French Army to victory, but she got burned at a stake for her efforts.

In nineteenth century China, families didn't bother to name their girls. Why waste a good name…they were called by their place in the family, e.g. "third sister" and that was good enough. Then to make that girl more attractive to men, her feet were crushed, broken and bound so that they couldn't grow. After time, her feet became three or four inch stubs, the "Golden Lilies" that were the epitome of fashion. Painful yes, but then she was a girl so it didn't matter.

## A Light in the Tunnel

The Society of Friends, aka "Quakers" were among the first to figure it out. In 1646 Founder George Fox rejected the popular notion that women had no souls.  He believed and preached that "God in every man" applied to women too. Modern minds find that comment self-evident.

George Fox didn't stop there. For him equality for women included education for girls. He set up Schacklewell School in 1688 to instruct young lasses and maidens in whatsoever was civil and useful. He was building on the slim history of girls' education first noted in ancient Rome where girls of all classes could attend the Ludus Publicus, the elementary school. Or he might have referenced the sporadic attempts at women's learning which occurred in the 12th Century when girls could be enrolled in "Convent Schools."

George Fox's enthusiasm for women's education had occurred way ahead of America's when Oberlin College was founded as a coeducational institution, in 1833. In 1837 four courageous women actually enrolled. More women's colleges opened, among them Mt. Holyoke, 1852 and Vassar in 1861. Hicksite Quakers founded co-ed Swarthmore in 1864.

It is remarkable and long overdue, that, after millennia of injustice, the time for women finally arrived in 19$^{th}$ Century America. Women's equality was deliberately included in the abolition movement. In July, 1848 two women, Elizabeth Cady Stanton and Susan B. Anthony said enough already, and organized a woman's rights convention in Seneca Falls, New York. They had a whole bundle of complaints to address: married women couldn't own property, if she worked, e.g. doing laundry, her wages belonged to her husband, in the rare event of a divorce the man had custody of the children. In no state, until Wyoming (1869) could a woman vote for other than possibly, a school board nominee. Lots of luck to those poor women who might want an advanced education. Most public universities were closed to women.

Brave souls rebelled against millennia of injustice, and in 1920 won "inalienable rights" for women too. But it wasn't easy. Courageous women prevailed through dreadful persecution since many people, mostly men, but some women too, opposed the liberation that women's rights would bring.

Not once, but twice, in the 1880's brave Belva Lockwood, ran for President of the United States. She was loaded with optimism since, being a woman, she couldn't vote anyway, not even for herself. But Belva wasn't the first woman to try for the presidency. Scandalous Victoria Woodhull ran in 1872 but missed the age cut-off by six months. And though there were other women candidates, it would be 144 years until another woman, Hillary Rodham Clinton, would have a serious chance to be elected president. But this time denial came, not from the people, but from the Electoral College. In 2016 Hillary captured the popular vote by an almost three million vote majority.

The sexual harassment scandals which rocked 2017 ironically mobilized a long dormant women's rage for justice, and propelled their sisterhood into the #MeToo movement. No way now to head off the juggernaut that is millennia long overdue. Equal Rights for Women is not fully birthed, but its head is definitely showing. In 2018 Midterm Elections, inspired by women's marches, and perceived injustice in a Supreme Court nomination, a record number of women, 272, ran for election to the U.S. Congress. In January, 1919, 126 women served in the 116th Congress of the United States.

_____

# Chapter 2
## Chrysalis Alice

Ruthless, dictatorial, elitist and devoid of personal connections. Words occasionally used to describe Alice by coworkers in the suffragist movement. But really? True, she had no patience for women who whined. She herself could and did embrace adversity. For Alice, discomfort was collateral damage for a successful movement.

True she could have laughed more. She did in the beginning, but Alice was serious about winning votes for women, and the quiet charisma she grew into attracted and held an army of devoted women. She didn't engage in small talk; when others despaired, Alice made lemonade. Her wry little sense of humor, and a light in those steely blue eyes said it all; she'd probe all her boundaries. She was the dependable, go-to grown-up who still loved to dance.

And no matter what else, she dressed well and stayed in touch.

### Alice and How She Got That Way

Alice's personality reveals itself in her actions more so than her words. Hers was a wild ride which began ever so quietly in the peace-filled haven of a Quaker enclave in New Jersey. In later life Alice remarked that she had practically no ancestor who wasn't a Quaker. Her mother Tacie Stokes Parry traced her prestigious ancestry through Grandfather William Parry, co-founder of Swarthmore College, and further back to William Penn, all Quakers, famous or not. Her father, William Paul, orphaned as an infant, spent a youth shunted from family to family to boarding school and finally as a teacher in a Quaker school. But he followed the Quaker tradition of honest financial achievement and left teaching to enter business. His wealth increased with time and when Alice was born, he was a wealthy man, owner of a 600-acre New Jersey estate.

Unlike so many of her contemporaries outside the Quaker community, Tacie Parry attended college, of course Swarthmore. In mid nineteenth century America a mere 2% of American women were so lucky.

But when William Paul entered her life she left before senior year to wed. Married women were not allowed in school. To be united, she and William recited the simple Quaker vow, one sentence promising faithfulness and love, so different from then current vow "to love, honor and obey." With five older brothers Tacie Parry had learned to hold her own in conflict and her marriage did not end her activism. She continued her membership in the local women's suffrage group and stuck strictly to the ideal of equality in her marriage… mostly.

With their diligence and unrelenting work habits, Quakers in America had succeeded so as to put the community at odds for the avowed Quaker tradition of simplicity. But its message was not lost on Tacie Paul. She dressed in the unadorned manner considered appropriate. Her thick dark hair was kept tidy in a bonnet, standing high at the crown, and extending close along the sides. Dull shades of brown or grey were favored, though an occasional muted red provided a bit of variety. Plain buttons or a line of hooks and eyes closed the bosom of the dress and one more hook and eye, anchored a capelet to her shoulders.

Into this Quaker cocoon on an unusually warm winter's day, January 11, 1884, the chrysalis, Alice, was born, a sweet baby girl whose DNA seethed with the seeds of a rebel, and the cunning of a vixen. She would move far and fast, as she grew, but that violent future was unknowable then to Tacie and William, as they welcomed their first born. Now prosperous, they had just moved into the gracious old farmhouse that was Paulsdale.

For two years, Alice would be their only child, absorbing the reserve of both parents, and the rigid standards of her father. Though man and woman were equals in a Quaker marriage, reality was often different. Some thought that Tacie feared the formidable William since he brought prosperity to the family, but lacked affection. His difficult upbringing did not allow him to display emotions. Alice's promise, however, was not lost on him, prophesizing "When there is a job to be done, I bank on Alice."

The Paul's home, a commodious old farmhouse nestled in a wooded plot, resounded with the antics of the three children who followed. Brother Will joined Alice in October, 1886, Helen the following year and another boy, Parry in 1895. So, the ranks were swelled for the games that abounded, checkers on the wraparound front porch and tennis on the court carved out on the front lawn. Winter brought sledding on the lawn's slope and skating on frozen ponds. Unusual for their times, the Quakers encouraged athletics for girls and Alice took every advantage.

The children scarcely noticed that there was no music, or card playing allowed in their home. Such activities were considered a distraction from work. Alice later recalled that she didn't regard it as oppressive, because she just didn't know there was such a thing. And furthermore, music and dancing were considered the failings of less worthy people. Referring to the Irish maids who lived on the home's third floor and worked for the Paul family, Alice remarked, "gay maids" …who attend dances where music was played-*music-*

suggested hidden pleasures. [2] They went off to dances and just lived a different life from the Pauls' who felt that it was only "common" people who did such things.

The problem with their Quaker cocoon is apparent; no one questioned their own notion of superiority. Their spirit of egalitarianism did not apply outside the Quaker community. The Paul family was a member of the Hicksite Quaker Community whose precepts demanded the use of "thee" and "thou" and "thy" in addressing one another. "You," and "your" smacked of superiority. Remarkable sensitivity, considering their contempt for Catholics and "other."

But the late nineteenth century *Friends Rule of Discipline*, had loosened up and no longer prohibited nursery rhymes and tales and the Paul family allowed Alice unlimited access to the books they collected in their library. Alice read and then reread their complete collection of Dickens whose commentary on social ills probably influenced her later acute sense of social justice.

## A Very Long Journey/ The First Step

Being Alice, already a confident six- year-old girl athlete, she walked or rode her bike the one-mile trek to Moorestown Friends School. Later she would arrive riding her horse bareback. It cost big money to attend Moorestown Friends, seniors paid $1.25, but non-Quakers were accepted and that steep price kept the student body rather exclusive.

Alice's earliest school photo has the little girl's hair in Quaker style, severely pulled back past her ears and parted in the middle. Her school clothes are more colorful than her mother's drab style. She wears a plaid blouse under a long, white cotton jumper. Tidy black lace-up shoes complete the

---

[2] Walton, Mary, *A Woman's Crusade,* (New York, New York: Palgrave Macmillan, 2010), p. 5

outfit. Her lovely dark eyes are serene; she knows she has this school business under control.

In the Hicksite tradition, girls and boys took their classes together but were strictly forbidden to fraternize otherwise without supervision. The prevailing mentality of most women's rights activists of the times was that girls and boys were "different" with girls holding the moral superiority. Later this notion would be used as a talking point for women's suffrage and used to exclude them from "dirty" politics.

High school sees Alice a young woman now, her chestnut hair dark and lustrous, her deep set, startling blue eyes serene. She smiles little, hiding her teeth which protrude slightly. Buried below her calm exterior is the tension she will bear through life. She will approach challenges struggling to excel and experiment, often scared to death, but resolute in purpose.

So Alice, always on the prowl for a challenge, took up high school athletics with her usual intensity. She added basketball and hockey to her skill set, taking advantage of the Hicksite Quakers' support of vigorous exercise for women. At her time sports for women were generally derided by society at large, since girls were deemed too delicate for vigorous activity. Later life would have Alice drawing on this early physicality; her stamina would be sorely tested in both English and American prisons.

For now, though, life was good, So many challenges; so little time. Her course load was heavy, tilted towards languages: four years of Latin, three each of German and French. But the curriculum also included math, science, composition, history and drawing, then there was the literary magazine and the debating team, a tough job for a shy girl, and the Quaker suffrage meetings with Tacie. Ironically, the cause which would shape her life left her rather bored at that time.

She was busy cramming for finals. Last minute learning was her style.

Then there was reading, her ultimate passion. Once again, society would attempt to contain girls.  Defying the prevailing mentality which cautioned that too much reading would damage the delicate adolescent female brain, Alice read voraciously. She especially enjoyed biographies of exceptional women like her fellow Quaker and early advocate for women's rights Lucretia Mott and her life-long role model, Florence Nightingale. Her taste in literature was fortunate because till 1895 the library banned any novels, romances or works of a suspected immorality, Thomas Hardy's *Tess of the d'Urbervilles* would never make the cut.

So as her teen time passed, Alice continued to excel, a fact which surprised no one. Alice always knew she could pull it off, she knew she was that smart, and she did, graduating high school and entering Swarthmore College at age 16.

# Chapter 3
## Swarthmore and Liberation

Today's college acceptance letters don't look like Alice's. Swarthmore's Dean of Women, Elizabeth Bond wrote to the Pauls "...it is desired that thy daughter have permission to attend only such social gatherings as are approved by the faculty." She continued, "that permission to visit the city shall not include the privilege of attending the theatre with the young men of the College." [3] Nevertheless, though a Hicksite Quaker college, some liberties were allowed. Dress was more colorful, bonnets were doffed and music was permitted, women's dancing, also, but never with men.

So it was on a rainy day in September, 1901, that Alice arrived at Swarthmore College, after a short railroad ride from Philadelphia. Out from under her umbrella she surveyed the stately, four storied Parish Hall that would be her haven, and beyond to the women's gym, meeting house and science building half hidden in mist.

Lucky Alice, with money and connections was enrolled in Swarthmore when in 1901 95% of college age women, didn't go. Many questioned the value of educating women, since a great portion of such women remained single. This "New Woman" who emerged often aspired to a meaningful job, and she was generally unpaid because proper women did not work for money. Leave that to the low class

---

[3] J.D. Zahniser & Fry, Amelia R., *Claiming Power,* (New York, New York: Oxford University Press, 2014), 15

types, and teachers too, maybe. Tuition at Swarthmore was steep, $400. per year and the student body remained elite.

With an eye toward frugality, Alice chose a less expensive room far back in Parish Hall's third floor. She didn't choose her roommate, though, and wasn't impressed or even especially kind to Edith Powell, another 16-year-old freshman awaiting her. Alice as yet bore the results of the limited exposure of her privileged upbringing and couldn't tolerate Edith's Eastern Maryland speech or her social awkwardness.

But Alice moved in and unpacked her clothes, rather showy and fashionable now. Frugality aside, her clothes were off the rack, not the traditional Quaker homespun that Tacie favored. Alice liked red for class and casual. Her tops were the currently popular shirtwaists worn by working women, a high class slumming style. Shirts were worn with ankle length trumpet skirts, a bell shaped fashion still available on line today. But dinner was a formal affair and students dressed well.   Alice, always clothes minded, favored gauzy white cotton or linen dresses.

## Alice Unleashed

Swarthmore was Alice's alternate universe. And being Alice, she reached out to its possibilities with joy.  On the first page of her freshman diary she recorded a reception hosted by upper class women. "The old girls sang the Swarthmore songs and then we went over to the gym to dance. Danced whole evening and had a glorious time."[4] Yes, she was dancing with women, still, she'd come a long way from Moorestown

---

[4] Walcott, *A Woman's Crusade*, p. 8

---

where no one danced with anyone; dancing was strictly forbidden.

Some mixing of the sexes was allowed in the safe environs of the dining hall. Conversation was encouraged among the women and men who ate their meals together, but always under the cautious eyes of the professor present at the table.

Alice recorded her dining experiences, quite thrilled with the ritual. She described the way students processed into the room, "You all came in together, then the boys arose and went out and brought in the food and placed it on the table."[5] No privilege here for the males, women would be served by men in cutting edge Swarthmore. Although she initiated a coed social hour after dinner, Dean Powell kept a close eye on intermingling of the sexes. Girls were not to be seen outside their east wing and certainly not in the hallways and parlor.

But academic barriers did not exist. Girls and boys were admitted to Swarthmore in equal numbers, and no course of studies was denied to either sex. Alice chose biology for what was possibly all the wrong reasons. It wasn't like she intended to use biology; as a "respectable" woman she wasn't planning a career. Alice was a literary type, invested in print not test tubes. "...the one thing I don't know anything about, and I never would read and I can't understand it or comprehend it or have any interest in it are all the things in the field of science...so I decided to make biology my major...but then there was chemistry, and physics and higher mathematics... I didn't do too well in them...these classes were almost all young men

---

[5] Zahniser, Fry, *Claiming Power*, p. 17

students because they were all studying to be engineers and took it very seriously.[6]

Alice's study habits hadn't improved much in college, and given her punishing required course load: math, biology, chemistry, bible literature, French, and composition (she added art and elocution [speech]. She was clearly a quick study. It's telling that although she had no practical use for her major, she persisted and eventually graduated with straight A's, only Chemistry, a B.

Life for Alice at Swarthmore was a delightful escape. She met men students, but mostly befriended women. So far removed was she from her sober Paulsdale upbringing that she fell under the sway of Rena Miller, a charming and creative fun lover. Playing pranks, using the gas light jets to cook up fudge, sneaking out at night, all gave Alice release from her somber beginnings. Following the nineteenth century custom of women sharing beds, Alice kept a list of the women she slept with, though no intimacy other than friendship was ever recorded. Irrepressible Rena's name probably appeared often.

Somehow she was even able to fit sports into her crushing academic and social life and donned the bloomers, loose trousers gathered at the ankles, now allowed to women athletes.  Amelia Bloomer knew "…how ready and anxious women were to throw off the burden of long, heavy skirts." [7] Alice joined the basketball team, played tennis, skated on frozen Crum

---

[6] *Conversations with Alice Paul,"* interview by Amelia Fry, Suffragists Oral History Project, Bancroft Library, Berkley University, College and Social Work, 1975, 27

[7] National Women' History Museum  Search  Amelia Bloomer

Creek, danced, still ladies only, rowed,  hiked and even with all that managed to put on 12 pounds. Might have been too many late night fudge sessions.

## The Party's Over

But some events interfered with Alice's delightful free fall. It wasn't long before her antics were reported home and she had to see less of Rena. Tacie and William might also have been apprised of the fact that their daughter was sometimes skipping Quaker First Night Meetings and was accompanying friends to non-Quaker churches. Throughout life Alice actually did remain ambivalent about formal Quaker rituals but its fairminded principles were her innate frame of reference, guiding her through the horrendous injustices she would encounter.

Then in late April, 1902, sad news arrived. A pesky cold had developed into pneumonia, and in short time William Paul was dead.  Alice rushed home to Paulsdale and into a life changed. William had done well with his various enterprises and banking job, so Tacie's financial prospects were good, but she must manage the family alone now.  Her children could be less inhibited; Will and Parry more outgoing. Tacie acting boldly, bought Helen a piano. There would be music in the home. Of her four children, Alice had been most exposed to William's steely resolve and maybe carrying that part of him as herself allowed her to deal with his early death.  And maybe, living longer under William's intense presence, Alice might be a less inclined suffragist.

A week later she returned to Swarthmore, and picked up where she left off, spending her freshman days with close friends, and participating in athletics, debating and literary societies. Sophomore to Senior years were a blur of pleasant experiences and daunting studies. Barriers were dropping, students had more freedoms. "Progressive" professors introduced new ideas about social and political reform.

Alice's Swarthmore idyll ended in senior year, 1905, and she supposed she would teach… or not. There was money enough in the Paul household, so that earning a living was not all that important. Her pre-med major in biology had been mostly to prove a point since she actually had little regard for doctors.

Anyway, the times were changing. A phenomenon burst. The wondrous "New Woman" emerged and never looked back.

# Ready to Roll! A Lady's Safety Bike,1885

## *Lagniappe: The "New Woman"*

The "New Woman" didn't much resemble the old woman. For starters, she was on wheels a lot, real wheels, bicycle wheels, and she was wearing pants, Bloomers!

Plainshumanities.unl.edu

She'd shucked the corset for the long pants popularized by Amelia Bloomer, sometimes worn under a shorter skirt. Now she could play basketball, and tennis and golf but mostly it is contended, it was the freedom to ride her bike that contributed most to women's liberation.

At least that's what Founding Mother, Susan Anthony believed. "I think it has done more to

emancipate women than anything else in the world."
Not only did she now have control over her
transportation, but she was free to dress and behave in
ways that shattered traditionally held visions of women.

Actually biking freedom was just fallout from
an evolving social earthquake. Seismic forces had
collided, and from that blast the "New Woman"
emerged. After over 2,000 years, the Juggernaut that
was Women's Rights exploded and tipped off, rolled
over and out. Circumstances always make for change,
but the late 19th Century, beginning with the
Industrial Revolution, fomented women's perfect storm
and the unthinkable occurred. There was more than
unpaid house and farm work available to women.

Though the jobs created were generally either
awful or domestic or both, women were finally earning
their own money. By early 1910 the number of women
employed had risen to 7.8 million. Some, though
largely not welcomed, were able to infiltrate the male
bastions of law and medicine. Starting with Emma
Gillette (1852-1927) who was denied admission to law
schools because of her gender, but was accepted at and
graduated from Howard University. Elizabeth
Blackwell, rejected by every school in Philadelphia, by
Harvard, Yale and Bowdoin, in 1849. Finally the male
students prevailed and Geneva Medical College in New
York granted her a medical degree. She was the first
America woman physician.

Another happy collision was the intersection of
women's education (See Appendix) with electricity. In
the late 1800's electric stoves, clothes washing
machines, irons, vacuum cleaners freed women from

the exhausting labor of maintaining the required "perfect cleanliness." African American Josephine Cocoran invented the first commercially successful dish washing machine. With more free time now, women worked outside the home, and some even moved out of the house. Then the War came and women were needed to join the military to relieve soldiers from clerical duties. The Yeomen (F), the first female yeomen, served the U.S. Navy in 1916 though most still unable to vote.

The typewriter was the New Woman's escape method of choice, and by 1900, according to the census, 94.9% of typists were unmarried women. With their own money in their own pockets, these free souls were able to hang out in some places that were suspect in polite society. But the "New Woman" was having too much fun at Dance Halls and amusement parks to give a hoot about public opinion.

# Chapter 4
## It Seemed Like a Good Idea at the Time

So, in fact, Alice's amazing career trajectory blasted off accidentally. She signed up for the required political science and economic classes offered in her last year at Swarthmore and surprised herself by loving them. Her professor, Robert Brooks, recognized her potential, and rewarded her with a scholarship. She could live expense free in a settlement house for one year acting as a resource to the local community.

### A Delicious Bite of the Big Apple

Alice chose New York City and moved to the College Settlement House, "The major purpose of the settlement house was to help… immigrants into the labor force by teaching them middle-class, American values."[8]located deep in the heart of a Jewish and Italian immigrant neighborhood. There, at 95 Rivington Street in New York's lower East Side, the atmosphere was electric. The street vendors, the music, the food…the filth, so very different from her staid Quaker culture.

---

[8] Harvard University Library Open Collections Program, *Immigration to the United States, 1789-1930* [9] *Conversations with Alice Paul*, p. 30

---

But immersed in the field of social work, feisty Alice became impatient. "By the time I was there for a while, I knew I didn't want to be a social worker, whatever else I was." Clearly, her destiny. lay elsewhere. "...to spend all your life doing something that you knew you couldn't *change* the situation by social work."[9] Obviously Alice had no problem sharing her feelings.

Though she professed to disdain social work, typical of Alice she performed it with gusto. "...you got to know the city of New York in places which were sort of the underground places, - not *underground*, but the under layer of people who were up against it. So all summer I stayed there."[9]

So with her heart in the right place, but her head elsewhere, she followed her gut feelings and in the fall of 1906, left town for the University of Pennsylvania and graduate school. She'd learned that the sources of power laid in politics and economics. Now Alice had the solution; the cause would present itself shortly.

In grad school, Alice majored in government and those classes were almost exclusively male. Her observation of the dominance of males studying the areas of political power must have filtered into her consciousness somewhere, but right now she was just a sponge for ideas. For fun she'd go on to study in Europe as she'd found a Quaker Study Center in Birmingham, England. Her Quaker supporters could foot the bill.

---

[9] Ibid,30

## Europe Meet Alice

So Alice cut out early. She skipped U. Penn graduation, packed up and shipped out for Europe. She'd do Germany for the summer and be in Birmingham come fall.

Fall 1907, found Alice on the road again, by train, then boat, then train to Woodbrooke and more graduate studies at the University of Birmingham. Just four years old, (and still going strong) the Quaker Study Center Woodbrooke [10] had grown from chocolate; George Cadbury had donated his old home to serve as a center for Quaker thought and action. Alice cheerfully located herself among the assorted students, male and female, mostly American and to her, rather lackluster.

Few could match Alice. Adding to her Woodbrooke course load, thrice weekly, Alice pedaled her bicycle through the choking factory produced coal fog, to classes at the university, studying economics. Looking around, Alice found herself the lone woman in her chosen field of study. "I am the first woman who ever took a course in the whole department of commerce at this Univ." [11] With a bit of buyer's remorse, she thought maybe she should have studied Greek or something more feminine.

But not really, Alice was following her heart. Deep down, even unacknowledged, she was firmly convicted of social justice, and somehow she knew the path to true equality lay in the reality of economics and politics. Her actions gave the lie to her condemnation of

---

[10] Woodbrooke.org.uk/
[11] Zahniser& Fry , p.45

social work. In her spare time, between schoolwork and revived athletics, tennis, biking and ice skating, she took on part time employment at a settlement house; it was what she knew.

### Alice Meet Christabel

Then something happened which tripped off the arc of Alice's life. It was a public meeting at the university, and an ordinary event in the student calendar. Sir Oliver Lodge, the university president, regularly invited speakers, often undistinguished, to present on a variety of topics. That afternoon, a woman named Christabel Pankhurst, would speak on the topic "Votes for Women."

Alice described her reaction to Christabel Pankhurst. "Anyway she was a very young girl and a young lawyer, one of the few women that had ever studied law I guess in England at that time. Quite entrancing and delightful person, really very beautiful I thought. So she started to speak. And the students started to yell and shout, and I don't believe anybody heard one single work that Christabel said. So she kept on anyway for her whole speech. She was completely shouted down. So I became from that moment very anxious to help in this movement. "[12]

Sir Oliver Lodge was vitally provoked. Student protest was not appreciated under his watch. He held the trashing of his invited speaker as a great disgrace to the university and apologized to Christabel. She was invited for a return performance, and this time attendance was required and he would be there. Now, at her rerun, the young lawyer, speaker, suffragette had

---

[12] *Conversations with Alice Paul* , p. 41

---

a rapt audience. Somehow, Sir Oliver's looming presence seemed to encourage good manners from his rowdy male students.

So it was all over for Alice. All that thinking, all those Quaker ideals, the settlements, the wandering finally made sense. "Well then I understood everything about what the English militants were trying to do. She and the other young women who spoke with her- they were all three young girls- they had anyway one heart and soul convert...that was myself... all there was to it. [13]

But later Alice would have to ask herself, could she pay the terrifying price of Christabel Pankhurst's cause? Maybe she hadn't come so far. Maybe she would just go home and make her mother happy.

Or maybe not.

---

[13] Ibid. 41

# Part Two: Metamorphosis (1906-1910)

## Chapter 5
## Suffragettes Get Nasty

Christabel Pankhurst's doll-like appearance was deceptive. Beneath her curls and big, blue eyes burned a crafty and fearless mind. Years before her appearance at Birmingham, Christabel and a friend had deliberately interrupted a political gathering, shouting "Votes for Women." When a police officer threatened her, she deliberately kicked him and spit in his face, a guaranteed arrest, followed by a week in jail.

That was just what she had intended. Christabel played the "innocent" card, a "victim of police brutality" and with the publicity she attracted, she breathed new life into the flagging English suffrage movement. Jail terms for women became a strategic weapon.

Christabel had learned defiance at home. Her mother, Emmaline Pankhurst was both the source of her three daughters' beautiful faces and also their bold behavior. She herself was a dismal failure at proper "ladylike deportment," and taught her daughters to be just as naughty. Their mother had good reasons for being concerned about women's rights. Her role as a Poor Law Guardian exposed her to the misery of women at the Chorlton Workhouse and convinced her that injustices would not stop until women could have a voice, a vote.

---

The status quo just didn't work for Emmaline. She had seen strident activism work for men. Current suffrage groups were simply too polite for her, so she and the girls, Christabel, Sylvia, and Adela, started their own movement. No more nice girl; they'd get ugly, and the Women's Social and Political Union (WSPU) was born. In winter 1907 They marched over and over to the seat of government, attempting to force their way inside. They just wanted to be heard. Met always by a solid phalanx of police the women were battered and bruised but persistent.

*Angry Emmaline in Action*

The horrified press, to distinguish this rowdy bunch from more sedate suffragists, nicknamed them "suffragette." The female suffix intended as a slur, an implication of weakness.

They gladly accepted the name. They were tough women, and didn't much care what you called them.

Emmaline Pankhurst had promised the greatest demonstration London had ever seen, and she kept her word. The hype began ten days early. Women chalked announcements on sidewalks, rang doorbells, passed out flyers on street corners, and actually hired 30 trains to transport the out-of-town crowd.

Even the weather knew better that to mess with Emmaline, so it was on a beautiful spring day that the ladies stepped out. With exquisite pre-planning, not one, but seven separate parade contingents appeared simultaneously, pouring out from London's streets, a wave of cheering women bearing banners, and pennants and flags and shouting and marching relentlessly for their rights. Illuminating a sea of white dresses, the sun beamed on their dedicated colors: purple (wisdom), white (purity) and green (hope). This astonishing spectacle would climax when the seven processions joined forces at their rallying point, London's famous Hyde Park.

Alice's heart burst with pride as she marched. All those years of learning in schools and in social work had really been the crucible of this glorious moment. This joyous outpouring of purpose was Alice's epiphany. She could see clearly that her life's work was the cause held so dearly by this fearless band of women. "… on this occasion, I became a member of the Women's Social and Political Union. You became a member by signing an application blank and giving 25 cents…I was just so *extremely* happy to really be a part of it." [14]

Lady Pethick-Lawrence, editor of a left-wing newspaper, marshalled Alice's section and as they entered Hyde Park Alice could see the platforms raised and ready for the day's speakers. "I didn't know where I was going. I just walked where I was sent. …The other people were surrounding another platform, just by chance I had her platform. …She was a great, great speaker I thought. And so I became sort of again linked with what I had heard of in the University of Birmingham.[15]

And when it was finished at Hyde Park, when all the speakers had spoken there sounded a bugle blast, and all present cried out with one voice, "Votes for women, votes for women!" Though the women's battle cry resounded across London, unfortunately the

[14] *Conversations with Alice Paul* , p. 45
[15] Ibid. 44

Members in Parliament just heard more noise from a mob of silly women.

So life went on for Alice, and always a student anxious for facts, she would find work at the Peel Institute, and enroll in the London School of Economics. Her salary was small and her wardrobe was outdated, a distinct disadvantage in discriminating London society. Fortunately for Alice, Tacie had money and her support was crucial. Alice wheedled $50. from her mother, quit her job, found a roommate and became a full-time student again.

Thereafter, Alice also became increasingly an activist, faithfully attending WSPU meetings and at the behest of LSE fellow student Rachel Barrett she found herself standing on streets, hawking the WSPU newspaper, *Votes for Women.* This action was not natural to Alice. During the march she had been surrounded by others, and now she was alone. As she stood there, forced by Vendor Law to stand in the gutter and calling out, she needed all her courage. The public and cab drivers were not always polite, often deliberately splashing her. But in spite of her fears, she showed up regularly and such grit caught the eye of the WSPU leaders. Timid Alice was asked to speak publicly, a task which had paralyzed her at Swarthmore. Now she was seasoned and they rewarded her with a soap box and a street corner for her venue. After a while Alice was everywhere speaking on corners and in parks, standing aloft and doing well.

Then everything fell apart. Tacie had three other children to raise and wasn't anxious to send her daughter, the perpetual student, more money. She did, but indicated that she must come home and educate herself locally. Then Alice's teeth went bad, and she broke her glasses, and the landlady upped the rent. Matters couldn't get worse; unless they did. A letter arrived from Swarthmore informing her that the scholarship she had applied for had gone elsewhere. Alice, was heartbroken and depressed, and even stopped attending class.

But then everything changed again, a note arrived from WSPU with an invitation for a deputation to the prime minister himself and probably, as a result, she would go to prison too.

She'd have good company in the lock-up, Emmaline Pankhurst was leading the charge in person. Nevertheless, Alice was not to respond unless she was willing to be arrested and thrown in jail.

Now Alice was truly in crisis. Prison wasn't the problem; Quakers had gone to jail before. It was her mother's and her family's reputation which might suffer in polite society. Maybe she'd go under an assumed name, cut her hair, dress funny? Maybe she shouldn't go at all? Yes.

No,

Finally, yes… I suppose. So, she wrote the yes letter, but it made her head hurt. She walked around and walked around for days, the sealed envelope burning hot in her pocket; scared silly by the good chance that her future was doomed once she put her acceptance into the mailbox. Had she the nerve to follow her vision into hell?

Then she mailed it.

# Chapter 6
## No Votes for Women?  Food Fight!

Prime Minister Asquith was totally out of patience with the suffragettes; they kept saying the same old thing. *Women should have the right to vote*, a non-starter in his world. But English law allowed for the right of Deputation, i.e. Petition, and that's just what P.M. Asquith refused. Emmaline would take him out on that with the largest deputation of women yet. The suffragettes would publicize his intransigence and hopefully embarrass him.

Marion Wallace Dunlop went first. She was an artist and the indelible rubber stamp she affixed to Parliament building's main entrance announced the upcoming deputation tastefully, in shades of violet graffiti. Her neatly printed quote from the 1689 Bill of Rights said it all: "It is the right of the subject to petition the king, and all prosecutions for such petitioning are illegal." They arrested her anyway, for :
"willfully damaging the stone work of St. Stephen's Hall, House of Commons." Marion declared she was a political prisoner, not a vandal, and refused to eat until she was treated as such. The dishes of tempting meals offered her were thrown out her prison window. Pigeons feasted for 91 hours as she dumped out her

food. Prison authorities, fearful she'd die and become a suffragette martyr, released her. Lots of press ensued and thus was born the suffragette ultimate tactic…the hunger strike. Thanks to her, thereafter, the first response of an arrested suffragette was to refuse food.

WSPU ladies also knew the value of publicity. Marion Dunlop's arrest and hunger strike had brought attention and sympathy to their cause. Nevertheless, the women in the large protest should prepare for the worst. At their next march, they should anticipate shoving and pummeling by the police and should dress accordingly, e.g. big shirts and skirts with substantial padding beneath. They should waddle in waves toward the House of Commons. At 7:30 PM the streets around Parliament were packed with spectators, estimated at 50,000.

The Pankhursts were never spontaneous; every aspect of every protest and parade had been planned in minute detail and marchers were fired up that evening with a raucous preevent rally. Fife and drums blared, banners waved, and all around the packed Caxton Hall staging area, sashes and posters gleamed with the purple and white and green of the suffragette movement, though some set jaws and frightened eyes underlay the gaiety. The prospect of prison and its horrors was a reality. The women knew it could happen.

But then, at precisely 8:00 PM, June 28th, a black clad mounted horse woman announced the march and buoyed up by rousing cheers and a parade band, the first contingent stepped off. Emmaline had promised that Prime Minister
Asquith's refusal to grant an interview would force them "to use every possible effort to gain entrance" to the House of Commons and she meant it. They would

attempt entrance in waves and hers would be first. If they failed to get into the building, the second wave would follow and then the third and so on.

Waiting with her wave, caught up in the euphoria of the moment, Alice stood breathless in anticipation. Years later she'd channel the Pankhursts and rouse American suffragists with the song and pageantry and display she'd learned that night. But there on Victoria Street now, she was all about the suffragette. Jaws clenched, palms sweaty, so proud of the courageous women she followed, at that moment she knew she would follow her heart without question, wherever that might take her, whatever the cost.

Emmaline Pankhurst and her deputation of seven, pushed on through the crowds on Victoria Street and made it to the Parliament Square, now lined with some three thousand policemen. The government had planned well too. Each entrance to Parliament was blocked. Police officials escorted Emmaline's group to the Commons Doorway and there, an official informed them that Prime Minister Asquith would definitely not see them. Emmaline was resolute. "I am perfectly resolved to stand here until I am received." When a police inspector attempted to push the women back, she slapped his face. He knew she was trying to get arrested and refused to respond. So she slapped him again. That time it worked. It "worked" for Alice too.

The Pankhurst Plan called for successive waves of protesters. Alice described the scene in a letter home to her mother. "The suffragette threw themselves against the lines of police & forced their way through once or twice only to be captured in a few minutes. Behind them was the crowd yelling & shouting &

pushing them on but afraid to take part for fear of being arrested. The police grabbed the suffragette by the throats & threw them on their backs, over & over. "[16]

She continued "The mounted police rode us down again & again. Finally, when the police could not drive the women back or control the scene, the suffragette were arrested."

Busy hauling women to prison, the London Police were unaware of a stealth group of suffragettes. They were busting windows in government offices with petitions attached to rocks and slipping silently into the night. The London Police were playing hide and seek with bands of determined women.

## When Alice Met Lucy, BFFs

It was a bedraggled bunch of protesters that filled the police station, women barely conscious, their clothing shredded and dirty. But, to her amazement, among the crowds, Alice spotted a young woman wearing a tiny American Flag pin. Alice elbowed her way through the sad crowd and smiled happily at the only other American. She was Lucy Burns, a tall, beautiful red-head. Immediately they spoke, kindred spirts; they were in this mess together. Neither Alice or Lucy knew then, sitting in a mad London prison, just how their zeal would bind them together for years to come. Finally, at One AM, Parliament adjourned and the over 100 detainees were arraigned and released to await trial at a future date.

Back in New Jersey, Tacie Paul may have breathed a thankful sigh. Alice had written detailing her

---

[16] Zahniser & Fry, p. 70

arrest and asking for the money to buy a ticket home. She'd come just as soon as her trial was over. She'd go to school, get her doctorate and become a teacher. Tacie really should have known better. Her daughter Alice was born into Quaker righteousness; her forebears were heroes of revolutions.

Would Alice really turn her back on the flagrant injustice and willful abuse of the suffragette? The Pankhursts even offered to pay their fines if she and Lucy wanted to ship out to America before the trial. The two stayed and on July 9, Lucy and Alice awaiting their sentence, learned that the verdict was guilty with an appeal.

So Alice was on the loose again

Burns, Miss Lucy of C.U.W.S.(1917) LC-DIG-nec-09478

### Lucy Burns (1897-1966)

Lucy Burns was Alice Paul with a little more pizazz. With feet planted firmly in two worlds, Brooklyn and prison, she could disengage a bit. Sometimes during the American fight, to Alice's chagrin, she'd just take time off to go home to rest. But the same passion for a woman's right to vote sustained both of their indomitable responses to the prison terms and hunger strikes, and force feedings they endured.

Lucy's rap sheet read longest of the suffragists. She was sentenced to jail six times and proudly spent more jail time than any other suffragist. While in prison in 1917, it was Lucy who signed and sent the clandestine message through the holes around the jail cells' pipes. From cell to cell the tattered scrap of paper passed from woman to woman, asking each to declare herself a political prisoner, not a criminal. All of the women signed though aware of the dire consequences of their actions.

Doris Stevens who knew Lucy well described her this way: With her red hair like a flaming torch, and her body strong and vital, Miss Burns was the very symbol of woman in revolt. Without doubt, she possessed the voice of the modern suffrage movement-she could move the most resistant person with her emotional quality, and intellectual capacity. She was ideal for the stormy, courageous attack. [17]

Big, beautiful Lucy knew exactly how to lead. She hailed from Brooklyn, the fourth of eight siblings, in a warm and wealthy Irish Catholic family. After graduation from Vassar, and a brief stint as an Erasmus High School English teacher, she went on to study at Yale, and Oxford Universities. True to form, it was in an English jail that her fateful encounter with Alice Paul kicked off the most successful partnership in suffragist history.

## The Scottish Caper

The Pankhursts knew talent when they saw it and wasted no time. The twosome was invited to travel

---

[17] Stevens, Doris. *Jailed for Freedom*, p.78

to Scotland, for some serious disruption. A young cabinet minister named Winston Churchill was planning to speak.

With such a tempting offer Alice figured she'd get there and back before her ship sailed. A quick protest, some fun with the guards, and she was out of there. But her ship sailed on Wednesday, and she didn't get back to London till Tuesday. Not nearly enough time to gather her belongings and leave town.

Did Alice really think she could run up to Scotland, cause trouble and be back for the sailing? Or just maybe she planned it that way. She could express some regret and have a good excuse to stay some more. Anticipating her mother's chagrin, she got her money back at once and then immediately signed up for the next disruption.  Now a "Heart and Soul" convert to the suffragette mission, she wouldn't be seeing New Jersey soon again.

Being a Pankhurst Pick had certain advantages for Alice and Lucy. They rode to Scotland in the Pankhurst "Motorcar" and were chauffeured by, to their amazement, by a woman. Furthermore, the brand new Austin was bedecked in the Suffragette colors. A green car with a purple stripe and white spokes said it all. They were trouble on wheels! The weather was fair, the skies blue; the Burns and Paul show was on the road, and Emmaline would furnish the entertainment.  First stop, the gritty city of Glasgow, known for its rebel mindset and ambivalence towards England, low hanging fruit and ripe for a ladies' demonstration. At the WSPU Headquarters, it was determined that Alice and Lucy would on the following night enter the St. Andrews Hall in which the Colonial Secretary, Lord Crewe, was speaking. There they should disrupt his event by becoming obnoxious, and yelling "Votes for Women"

That was all well and good with just one problem. The entry tickets read, "For Men Only." But that was Lord Crewe's problem. Suffragettes were good at crashing political parties; roofs and windows were legitimate entry points. Alice and Lucy set out to appear as innocent pedestrians while they would reconnoiter the St Andrews Hall site in search of possibilities.

Sadly, no easy access point presented itself. Each of the four entrances was heavily guarded and the three stories of sheer sandstone walls precluded climbing. However, the women spotted an adjacent construction site at a library. With some promising materials, they could pile this piece on that piece and gain window access. Of course they would have to stay hidden on the roof till the following night when Lord Crewe would be available for disruption. They'd await the dark to hatch their plan.

A pale moon winked in and out of the clouds that August night. It was 1:00 AM. Alice and Lucy, shrouded in black cloaks, slipped through the deserted streets and disappeared into the shadowy construction area. A moist wind scattered the metal debris as agile Alice, still the athlete, climbed a narrow scaffold and gained the roof. It was all good. Lucy would follow and they would use their vantage place to open a window. They'd stay hidden on the roof till the following night when the windows would provide access and they could mess with Lord Crewe.

But a harsh voice cut through the air and Alice was startled by the night watchman's threatening words to Lucy. They demanded that she clear out in a big hurry. With no choice she did that and left Alice, wrapped in her black cloak, alone and hidden, on the roof of St. Andrews Hall.

At 2:00 it rained. Hard. She stayed on, displaying then the iron will that would not be moved no matter the cost to her body. At dawn, though buried in her wet cloak she was spotted there munching on chocolates. Later she recounted her chagrin.

"I was surprised to hear shouting and whistling, and looking up I saw a number of workmen watching me through one of the library windows. Pretty soon I saw someone climbing to the roof, and a workman made his appearance. I explained to him that I was a suffragette, that I wanted to get into Lord Crewe's appearance that night and I asked him not to give me away and also to request his mates not to do so.
The workmen behaved like bricks and took no notice of me."[18]

But Alice was disappointed when as the sodden sky brightened and another good hearted workman saw her and called the police to rescue her. Soaked and greatly distressed at her failure to disrupt the meeting, she was escorted from the site amid cheers from the crowd gathered to watch her removal. The remorseful informant apologized, so sad as to have exposed her.

Lord Crewe spoke later, his audience aware of the havoc reigning outside the doors of St. Andrews. The suffragettes were throwing themselves in waves against the locked doorways. The police were hauling them away. Alice, chilled and tired from her failed night on the roof, and Lucy, waving a "Votes for Women" banner were the first arrests. Emmaline, watching the scene, immediately posted bail.

[18] *Daily Record and Mail, 21 August, 1909*, Alice Paul Papers, 16:266

Daring Alice, always ready for a caper, was beginning to realize firsthand the heartless intransigence of the men in power. Steadily its effects would sober her, and shape her mind and her methods. Alice's moral parameters were finding themselves.

### Lagniappe: Suffragette Willing to Die for the Cause

Two other suffragette behaved outlandishly; both were willing to die for women's freedom. One actually did.

It wasn't Marion Wallace-Dunlop, (1864-1942) though she stated happily that her death in prison would definitely help the cause of suffrage. Her bold graffiti post in the June, 1909 protest, had earned her a month's stay in Holloway Prison. Immediately after she was sentenced, she demanded to be treated as a political prisoner and she stated "… as a matter of principle, not only for my own sake but for the sake of others who might come after me, I am refusing all food until this matter is settled to my satisfaction." [19] She thus established herself as the first hunger striker in recorded history.

Emily Wilding Davison (1872-1913) was the suffragette who died for the cause. A bright young woman, she took classes at Oxford University though they wouldn't admit to it. No degree was available for women at that time. Her teaching job was just too tame for Emily and she quit and joined up with the Pankhursts' suffrage movement. After a raucous protest in 1909 Emily found herself Manchester's Strangeways Prison. To resist feeding she barricaded

---

[19] Spartacus Educational.com/Wallace-Dunlop.htm

herself in her jail cell. So the prison officials hauled out the water hose and sprayed her until the cell's water level was six inches deep. Later she recounted her ordeal "I had to hold on like grim death. The power of the water seemed terrific, and it was cold as ice."

Maybe it was in the "Wilding" part of her name that shaped her, but Emily Wilding Davison, after prison, went on to protest and finally perform a foolish yet courageous act.[20] At the Epsom Derby, on June 4, 1913, with a round-trip railroad ticket in her pocket, and holding up two suffragette flags, she ducked under the fence and on to the track, facing the raging field of oncoming horses. Anmer, King George V's entry crashed into her before she could bestow her flags on him, a ridiculously futile misadventure. She died in hospital four days later, a madwoman to the press, a heroine in suffragette eyes.

---

[20] Ibid. Emily Wilding Davison

# Chapter 7
## Mission Accomplished

Every action has an equal reaction. Isaac Newton told us so and he was right. Alice Paul and Amelia Brown acted audaciously during the Lord Mayor's annual, most prestigious shindig. The reaction was swift and merciless, though not surprising. But, the price was cheap. Since they had infiltrated this most guarded event, the suffragettes would gain invaluable publicity.

Alice and Amelia were already hidden in place, when Lucy Burns began the plot by entering the hall on the arm of a "guest." They were a most attractive couple with Lucy's flaming red hair piled high, and her tall, handsome escort attentive to his companion. They both "so belonged," so young, so beautiful, so rich… they presented their credentials, which were so bogus.

The massive hall's air was electric, London's elite were all in attendance, alive, chatting and abuzz at the arrival of a rising star, Winston Churchill. Allowed inside now, Lucy saw her chance and seized the moment. With her Brooklyn brio in full swing, she stepped up close to Winston, waved a little suffragette flag and boldly confronted him. In a loud, demanding voice, she spoke her message. "How can you dine here while women are starving in prison?"[21]

Message delivered. She and her escort where thrown out of the hall.

Alice and Amelia took advantage of the party's excitement, crawling from their hiding places, they slipped upstairs to their vantage point in the glass enclosed balcony. They had to know that their plan to disrupt would be severely punished.

Feeling good about fooling the guards, perched above in the balcony's vantage point, shoe ready for action, Alice and Amelia awaited the perfect moment. Then it came, the room was hushed, the prime minister poised to speak. Suddenly, up above, a glass window was smashed and as the shards shattered below, two voices rang out, "Votes for Women, Votes for Women."

Though their mission was accomplished, a grisly ordeal awaited Alice when she was taken to the infamous Holloway Prison. But she had her mind made up even before the magistrate sentenced her to a month's hard labor.   No political prison status…no food. However, the jailors were on to the suffragettes now. So, you won't eat? They figured, we'll feed you. Now! And their distorted sense of justice produced inhuman treatment.

Twice daily Alice was taken from her bed wrapped in blankets because she refused to wear a prison uniform. A heavy matron mounted her waist and pinned her shoulders down. Matrons on each side held her arms. The doctor stood behind her and "pulled my head back till it was parallel to the ground. He held it in that

---

[21] Walton, p.30

---

position by a towel drawn  tightly around the throat & when I tried to move, he drew the towel so tight that it compressed the windpipe & made it almost impossible to breathe.[22]

Alice fought back and that brought out the worst in her captors.

At first they merely held me, but after a few times they tied me to a chair as my struggles made it difficult to feed me…. The tube very rarely went down the first time. It would usually go three fourths of the way through the head & then he would be unable to push it any further. …While the tube is going through the nasal passage it is exceedingly painful & only less so as it is being withdrawn. [23]

The forceful insertion of the nasal tubes abraded Alice nostrils and only after seeing the young woman's blood flow, ten days later, the doctor finally gave her a spray to deaden the pain. But the forced feedings continued. "Three times my head was held so far back that the tube came out between the lips instead of going down the throat. I then clenched my teeth and the doctor forced them open with some metal instrument."[24]

Not surprisingly, Alice doesn't relive the horrors of Holloway in her letters to Tacie, but generally unsympathetic American newspapers recounted her travails in lurid detail, accounts which must have agonized helpless Tacie, an ocean away. "There was an article that Alice was being forcibly fed & her screams could be heard all over the prison. I then

---

[22] Zahniser & Fry, *Claiming Power*, 99

[23] Ibid.,100

[24] Zanhiser & Fry, p. 101

felt that I must do something…to send a cable gram to American Ambassador, Reid, asking help."

Clearly the ambassador was more interested in solidarity with England than his duty to an American citizen. His reply supported Alice's imprisonment on the grounds that she was no better or worse than an English woman and deserved similar treatment. Alice's cruel, inhumane punishment appeared appropriate to Ambassador Reid. Or he just shut his eyes to injustice; aggressive women were socially unacceptable.

Twice daily for 55 days from November 9th, Alice was forcibly fed. Then on December 9, 1909 she was released from Holloway Prison. She'd served her 30-day prison term and with so much suffering Alice could quit the cause with honor. She'd done more than her part; she was an American fighting for English justice. She was weak, exhausted…and yet, amazingly she was unbowed.

No extremes of ill treatment had changed her. Somehow, the roots of those tough old Quaker forebears had combined with the intransigent suffragette spirit to produce an immovable object. Later that same day, in a voice small, but triumphant, Alice proclaimed, "I didn't give in."

In truth, Alice was on the edge of collapse. But the Pankhursts always took good care of their wounded and for a month, Alice rested in the stately home of suffragette sympathizers. There she plotted out her future. She'd stay in England for the January elections and then go home. She'd return to America and go to school. She'd get her doctorate and become a respectable teacher in a respectable profession for a respectable woman. She'd be dull. But then, they don't force feed teachers. She had a plan.

But so often the best laid plans just fizzle out.

## *Lagniappe: Hunger Strikes*

Definition: Merriman Webster: Noun: Refusal (as by a prisoner) to eat enough to sustain life.

Typically, a hunger strike is a non-violent tactic used to score political points or to affect a policy change by courting death to demonstrate devotion to a cause. Most hunger strikers will take liquids but not solid food. Irish hunger striker Bobby Sands (1981) took salt and water before he died after a fast of 66 days.

Hunger strikes might have originated in early Ireland as a night's fast on a landlord's doorstep to protest a violation of the custom of hospitality. It evolved into an effective form of protest in which guilt was attributed to the "oppressor".

Marion Wallace-Dunlop's hunger strike lasted 91 hours. She refused food until her captors, scared that she would die and embarrass them, released her, only a little more than three days into her sentence. Suffragettes caught on fast, and that's just what they did. Thereafter, immediately when jailed they would not eat unless they were given the rights of political prisoners. That tactic worked for a while. No one wanted dead women on their hands…and then they were forcibly fed with milk and eggs through tubes in their mouths and noses. In 1913 Parliament passed the law nicknamed the "Cat and Mouse Act" in which the hunger strike was tolerated until the prisoner neared death. The prisoner was then released and when she gained health, she was jailed again to finish her sentence.

## Physical Effects of Hunger Strikes

In 2007, in conjunction with the U.K. Department of Health, the British medical journal The Lancet published guidance on the management of hunger strikers. People who are in good health at the beginning of a hunger strike "are usually at little risk of dying from malnutrition for at least six to eight weeks," the guidelines state. But people who are ill can die from malnutrition in as little as three weeks. And if a person also refuses all fluids, including water, "deterioration is very rapid, with death quite possible within seven to 14 days, especially during hotter periods of the year."

At the beginning of a fast or hunger strike, hunger pangs usually disappear after two or three days, according to a document on mass hunger strikes from the California Correctional Health Care Services. Beyond 45 days, death is a very real risk, due to cardiovascular collapse or severe infection. Even after a hunger strike ends, refeeding has some real risks, since the metabolic changes that occur during severe fasting can be profound.

**More Information on hunger strikes can be found at the following resources:**

- Famous- People-who-went-on-a-hunger- strike
- Youtube " Iron Jawed Angels" Forced Fed Scene
- Temple of the Dog Hunger Strike
- Reddit.com/r/ Infographics "Hunger Strikes"

# Part Three: An American Journey (January, 1910-March, 1913)

## Chapter 8
## Welcome Home, Alice

Lucy stayed; Alice left, despite the Pankhursts' entreaties. They would pay her to stay.

But though she couldn't admit it, the horrors of Holloway had depleted her physically and mentally. After two and a half years in England, seven arrests, over 55 force feedings, and three jail terms, her indomitable spirit needed some time out, some rest and recreation... at home.

She departed England on January 5, 1910 congratulating herself that her ordeal at Holloway was a secret. No one other than Tacie could know of her mistreatment since she'd tried very carefully to keep her American identity hidden. "No one but Thee knows I'm coming.... I hope I will never see my name in the paper again." So, four days late, having been tossed about by an angry Atlantic, the *Haverford* docked in Philadelphia, and set out its gangplank.

As Alice emerged through the dusk into the brisk winter wind, Tacie saw her daughter for the first time in years. Alice was 25 now and a different woman from the high spirited adventuress she'd last seen. As ever, she was fashionably dressed, wearing a wide tricorn beaver hat and trim brown suit. She smiled happily at

Tacie and 15-year-old brother Parry come to welcome her home. But Tacie, with a mother's eye, saw the young woman's exhaustion and immediately planned for a quiet recovery among the comforts of her warm and very welcoming homestead, and so was Tacie scared by the parts of Alice that she could see had changed? Maybe.

Knowing her daughter so well Tacie had to sense a new iron resolve. She looked into Alice's clear blue eyes that didn't smile now, and worried all over again. Alice was trouble. Yet maybe while Parry giggled at his big sister's new British accent, life might still hold promise. Dark thoughts had no place at this happy reunion.

But then the reporters descended, and it all began again. Anonymous Alice was back in the news. For now, they just were looking to report the gory parts, though word had spread about the Pankhursts and their militant actions. Newsmen trailed the family to Moorestown, and Alice obliged with the truth of her ordeal, describing the force feeding episodes in graphic detail. "Something like vivisection," she explained, then added. "but if it ever becomes necessary for me to do it again, I shall do it without hesitation."

Alice personified conventional wisdom; *that which doesn't kill us makes us strong.* Jail didn't kill Alice, ergo…

# Chapter 9
## The Tenor of the Times in America

Two events illustrate the status of women in the early 20th century. One almost comical, the other a monumental tragedy.

President William Howard Taft agreed to deliver the welcoming address at the 1910 annual National American Women's Suffrage Association (NAWSA) convention in Washington. Though he was openly hostile to women's votes, the convention's organizers were a little surprised at his acceptance but thrilled to have him appear. He would open their event with warm wishes for its success. He would welcome the association's visit to D.C. His presence would endorse the NAWSA. It would be a win-win situation

Excited crowds gathered outside the hotel to catch a glimpse of the president. Except, at the opening session, he didn't appear. Everyone waited, and waited, growing restless and impatient until finally, the group's president, Anna Howard Shaw, reluctantly began to deliver her annual address. Half way through her talk, the doors opened and as the president's huge form silhouetted itself against the light, he paused for effect. Slowly he stepped forward and launched his enormous 340-pound bulk down the aisle amid fluttering white handkerchiefs, a traditional welcoming salute. No matter they had waited long, the president had arrived and they were glad.

The audience quieted in anticipation of an edifying address.

## President Taft and the Abuse of Power

But at the podium now, President Taft let loose, and opened a tirade, spewing venom and even a racial slur on the stunned audience. He mentioned that at one time he'd been in favor of women's suffrage, but had since changed his views.

"The theory that Hottentots or any other uneducated, altogether unintelligent class is fitted for self – government at once or to take part in government is a theory that I wholly dissent from." [25]

Oblivious to the audience's consternation, Taft plowed ahead with his nonsensical screed. The danger with granting women's votes was that "it may be exercised by that part of the class less desirable as political constituents and be neglected by many of those who are intelligent and patriotic and would be most desirable as members of the electorate.[27]

What was he thinking? Did he know who his audience was?

Then the hissing began and mounted until it permeated the room. Women couldn't vote against him, except in four western states, but they could still let him

---

[25] *Harrisburg Star Independent*, April 15, 1910, 8. [27] Ibid

know how they felt. So together they raised a mighty sound of disrespect.

Taft smiled. Like a forgiving god, he would overlook their girlish antics. Anyway, he knew his presidency was safe from women so long as they couldn't vote. He condescended to react to their disapproval. "Now my dear Ladies, you must show yourselves equal to self -government by exercising, in listening to opposing arguments, that degree of restraint without which self -government is impossible.[26]

Unfortunately, Anna Shaw just didn't "get it." In the year 1910 women were expected to know their place. They were held to a higher standard than men and hissing was to her an intolerable violation of their duty to be examples of civil behavior. Anna was mortified and on the next day called a successful vote on a NASWA resolution to thank the president for his appearance at the convention. Additionally, a letter was included condemning the disruption with sorrow, and denying any responsibility for the protest.

Taft graciously thanked them with an immediate response, "generously" disregarding the incident, and in effect, clearly dismissing women's political value. The suffrage movement was back to square one, still hoping that women's good manners and polite behavior would win them the vote.

### The Deadly Abuse of Owners' Powers

Then March 25, 1911 a fire broke out in the Triangle Shirtwaist Factory, in New York City, probably caused by a lit cigarette tossed into a bin of

---

[26] Ibid

dusty old fabrics. The blaze killed 146 garment workers, mostly newly arrived young Jewish and Italian immigrants, ages 16-23 who were paid $7.00 to $12.00 a week for working nine hours a day on weekdays, seven hours on Saturdays. [27]

The owners, Max Blanck and Isaac Harris, had four previous factory fires to their credit so it is thought the lack of a sprinkler system offered the possibility of yet another fire insurance payout. That day, as usual, the doors to the stairwells and exits were locked to prevent theft; managers routinely checked women's purses as they left. The foreman who held the keys had long since escaped. Likewise, the owners, visiting with their children, whose top floor offices allowed them access to escape on the roof.

Two valiant men, Joseph Zito and Gaspar Mortillalo continued to save lives by operating the elevators up to the ninth floor. That was before Mortillalo's elevator rails buckled under the heat. Desperate women jumped down the shaft, clinging to cables. But so many bodies landed on Zito's elevator that their accumulated weight made it inoperable.[28]

The fire raged through the factory's location, the seventh, eighth and ninth floors. New York Fire Department engines came screaming to the scene, and stretched their ladders to their highest extent – the sixth floor.   With exit doors locked, flames raging, no elevators, there was only the fire escape. But that hope

[27] Lifflander, Matthew L. *"The Tragedy That Changed New York"* New York Archives (Summer 2011)

[28] Triangle Shirtwaist Fire, Von Drehle, David, *"List of Victims"* Triangle, The Fire That Changed America. (New York, Atlantic Monthly Press, 2003)

died when the flimsy structure, twisted by heat and overload, just collapsed and dropped 20 victims 100 feet to the pavement.

In all 123 women and 23 men were killed, jumping out of windows or burned alive. But the shame of the Triangle Shirtwaist Factory Fire, one of the worst in U.S history, brought attention to the plight of workers and spurred the growth of The International Ladies Garment Workers Union. This movement finally brought reforms to women workers, though not everyone got the memo...two years later Max Blanck was arrested for locking the door in his factory. He was fined $20. Some asked why it took a great tragedy to correct injustice. Some might have wondered if it had.

## *Lagniappe: The Year 1912, Some Other Timely Facts*

Two more momentous events took place in 1912. One was frivolous but lasting: the other was just dreadful and disappearing.

On March 14, 1912, in the Chelsea section of Manhattan, the National Biscuit Company gave birth to and trademarked the OREO Cookie. Today, the site of its beginnings on Ninth Avenue, between 15th and 16th street is officially designated "OREO Way," a fitting acknowledgement of an American icon that checks in at 55 calories per. To enhance its appeal, in 1990, the filling's lard component was replaced by partially hydrogenated vegetable oil and now OREO Cookies can be enjoyed by vegans; no animal fat is included.

Why it is called "OREO" is anyone's guess, though rejecting French and Greek origins for the word, some claim it is simply short and easy to say. But, no matter its origin, the word is used internationally, OREO Cookies (there is no plural) garners about two billion dollars in annual sales. Some OREO ads reflect this worldwide consciousness, a blue, white and red filling was proposed for France's Bastille Day. However, some were upset and organized the OREO Boycott when its owner, the Mondelez Company, moved its factory to Mexico in 2015. Is there a jalapeno filling in the future?

Then the world learned on April 15, 1912, of a horrific tragedy. The Unsinkable *Titanic* was destroyed by the unthinkable, a collision with a North Atlantic iceberg.  The math was inevitable, 2,200 passengers and crew were supplied with 20 life boats, accommodating 1,178. 706 persons survived : First Class Passengers, 60%, Second Class, 42%, Third Class 25% and less than 25% of the crew, according to *Titanic Deconstructed*[29] Water entered the ship at an estimated seven tons per second and it took less than three hours for the world's greatest ocean liner to sink to the bottom of the sea. Captain Edward Smith went down with his ship.

The *Titanic's* final resting place is no secret, and there have been visits to the site of the wreck, 350 miles southeast of Canada's Newfoundland.  But unfortunately the indestructible Titanic was severed into two pieces, and defies its raising. Tourist excursions, seawater, shellfish and bacteria are devouring its remains. With time as its scattered parts

---

[29] YouTube *Deconstructing History*

---

disappear, the fabulous Titanic will exist only in tragic memory.

Yet, rising to the surface, Titanic 2, a functioning replica of the doomed ship, is planned to be bigger and better than its namesake. Titanic 2 is the dream child of Australian millionaire Clive Palmer, who envisions the lookalike as the flagship of his Blue Star Line. His Titanic 2 may be a happy maritime coda to a very sad song of the sea.

Bon Voyage!

# Chapter 10
## Alice is at it Again

Tacie thought Alice should rest and rebuild her ravaged body at home, in Paulsdale. She could nourish her with real food, good American cheese and bread and cakes and meat. She'd sleep in her own bed again, piled high with downy comforters, and maybe try out the formerly forbidden piano. Nestled into big old armchairs Tacie could see her oldest at home lounging before a roaring winter fire, maybe reading some poetry or some novels by Dickens.

And Alice did just that, - for a week. Newspaper reports of her Holloway Prison's abusive feedings had made her a celebrity at home, and suffragist supporters quickly found the way to Paulsdale. Out west the suffragists were getting bolder and the Philadelphia people wondered if their own movement could use a dose of militancy. Alice, with her history of active defiance in England, might be just the right go to person.

Immediately Alice was in demand, and the perennial question surfaced again. For many, mostly men, but women too, rigid expectations for women's behavior did not jibe with provocative public actions. Clearly, Alice had broken all the rules of decency when she'd allied herself with the notorious Pankhurst women. Acceptable women should stick to "pretty please."

Alice, happily agreed to an invitation to address the NASWA meeting in Philadelphia, and with deliberate prose, set the matter straight. "Do you think the suffragette like their own methods, or want to pursue violent tactics?" Her voice rose, "The price they are paying for their freedom is terribly dear, but they are convinced that only the methods of war and practical politics will ever win their cause…No one has ever been injured in the suffrage cause, except the suffragette." [30]  Philadelphia Chapter President, Jane Campbell approached Alice as she descended the podium. Alice recalled her comments. "because you are a figure now in the minds of people. Now we see what sort of a person you are and we'd like you to join on our committee…Then they formed a committee for the first time on having street meetings in Philadelphia and trying to make this movement better known.

So I was made chairman of the street meeting committee." [31]

So much for Tacie's rehab program.

Times were changing and some saw women's evolution as a plague. And some said it was about time. The reality was that women were simply becoming too educated, too outraged, and too energized to be repressed any longer. The old order was crumbling under the weight of its anachronism. Alice saw that and rushed to respond. In less than four months after her arrival home, Alice addressed the same 1910 NASWA Washington DC convention that President Taft had insulted.

---

[30] Zahniser & Fry, P.109

[31] *Conversations with Alice Paul* p.60

---

Jobs, created by the Industrial Revolution moved women into the labor market. But the exploitation of these people, generally defenseless immigrants, outraged social reformers and brought about the mandate for political solutions. Pressure from women voters would improve workers' conditions. Suffragists added the worker's cause to their own.

As the convention closed, Alice was probably part of the NASWA group which engaged in its useless annual Suffrage Hearings in the House and Senate. Anna Shaw and other leaders presented petitions with 404, 825 signatures to both houses. Shaw and other leaders then presented their case for the Suffrage Amendment. The congressmen thanked them profusely and closed the event until the same nonsense performance next year. No broken windows there. No progress either.

But maybe the NASWA's leadership wasn't unhappy that the Suffrage Amendment would once again be dismissed. Their plan called for a state-by-state approval of women's right to vote. They were hoping that a creeping implementation of suffrage would eventually suffuse the country, and that one morning Congress would wake up to a done deal. For Anna Shaw and her co-leader Carrie Chapman Catt, such a process would circumvent southern opposition, still smarting over the 15th Amendment granting black men the vote. These southern gentlemen had enough difficulty with a black man's vote and were adamantly opposed to empowering black women.

So now, though Alice was hanging with the heavy hitters, only she was carrying the bat. Society frowned on outspoken women. Back in Phillie, she drew upon milder British tactics to raise public

---

awareness of her cause. Broken windows, jail terms and forced feedings, were her frame of reference, so the American activists' chalked sidewalks. Holding open air meetings was Suffragists 101; but still nervy in some suffragists' minds. Anyway it was a start.

Then her old, "Partner-in-Crime," Lucy Burns came home for a visit, and the ladies took off their gloves.

### *Lagniappe: The Suffrage Amendment*

When our country was founded only one state, New Jersey, allowed women to vote. But they caught on fast and shortly revoked that right in 1807, and though women still couldn't vote in 1848, that was when matters finally began to change.

Several women were mad enough to step out and organize. Elizabeth Cady Stanton and Susan B. Anthony spearheaded the movement and gathered like-minded discontents in Seneca Falls, New York. They were an odd couple in appearance and personality. Elizabeth laughed easily and often. She was a large woman in body and in personality, a witty hostess, fond of good food and the mother of seven. Susan B. Anthony never smiled. Her photos show a grim woman, disciplined, single-minded in purpose. There was no room for a husband in a life devoted to women's causes, and it was in her name that the Suffrage Amendment was referred to as "The Anthony Amendment."

No matter their differences Stanton and Anthony shared daring and independence at a time when they and their loyal band of followers were vilified by society and excoriated in the press. The movement these two women initiated took 72 years to reach fruition. Sadly, neither one would ever live to vote, but the amendment they envisioned reads just as they would have it.   The Fifteenth Amendment prohibited denial of suffrage because of "race, color or previous condition of servitude." The irony of the fact was not lost on the women; immigrant men, recent arrivals, could cast a ballot, though women, lifelong residents, could not.

The Nineteenth Amendment, the "Anthony Amendment" adds to the Fifteenth, which in 1870 gave African American men the right to vote. Women could not be denied the vote because of their sex. The United States Constitution prohibits the states and the federal government from denying the right to vote to citizens of the United States on the basis of sex.

In November, 1920 in spite of their shiny new amendment, only about a third of eligible women turned out to vote. "Aunt Susan" would have had words with them.

———————————————

## Chapter 11
## Summer Fun

Alice had entered the doctoral program at the University of Pennsylvania, in early 1911 and had chosen her major. Most of the 90 women who were enrolled stayed with the Humanities. Not so Alice who, calling upon her Quaker notion of gender equality, waded fearlessly into male dominated studies.

So maybe it wasn't just her brains or her good looks or even her chic style that attracted suitors at the university. Maybe it was all of the above, but maybe it was her invasion of a man's world which stirred interest in Alice, especially among her professors. Though she might have accepted the occasional dinner invitation, it was the relationship with a Cornell Graduate (Karl) William Parker which took hold and persisted for years. Though William Parker would remain in her life, always quietly waiting in the wings, Alice chose to follow the paradigm of the "New Woman" whose dedication to a cause eschewed the distraction of marriage and motherhood.

After one semester of grad school, it was summertime in Phillie and Lucy Burns was back in town just in time to rev up Alice's old English engines of protest. Nationwide, impatient suffrage groups were becoming more outspoken, and the Philadelphia NASWA okayed summer open-air meetings. One organizer wrote, "No rent, no paid speakers (a luxury we indulged in occasionally) no notices to be sent to members, practically no expense at all."[32]

---

[32] Katzenstein, *Lifting the Curtain* 41

It was a win-win situation and the Burns & Paul Open Air show was on.  Alice was chair and she knew the drill. Maybe a little confrontation... maybe some jail time, a hunger strike was always good for publicity. Alice kicked off her campaign with an audacious move; her little band of merry protestors would demonstrate in a public place without asking for a permit. They'd just show up and begin speechifying. Hopefully, they'd encounter police opposition and make the newspapers. Alice and Lucy were hungry for action such as they'd experienced in England, but that day the police stopped by and only watched.

The summer of 1911, saw Alice sharpening her organizing skills. She juggled money, passed the hat at meetings, and for publicity sent women at night to chalk wake up "Votes for Women" sidewalk messages, as free advertisement. She recruited personnel (her no nonsense reply to a timid speaker, "We've all done that").[33]

By September 30 she was ready for the big time. Independence Square, Philadelphia, site of the birth of the Declaration of Independence and the United States Constitution, neither of which documents had addressed women's rights, but whose tenets proclaimed those rights the women now demanded. Alice had managed to reserve this revered space for a monster culminating rally. NAWSA Chair, Anna Shaw, becoming a reluctant convert to action, spoke on one of the five platforms. Big, beautiful, blonde and bold activist Inez Mulholland made the trip down from New York City and captivated the crowd. Clearly, Alice's

---

[33] Zahniser & Fry, p. 121.

summer protests had worked, and with an audience of about 2,000 she could congratulate herself.

That chapter closed now, she would return to her doctoral studies and the attentions of her professors and mentors and William Parker.

# Chapter 12
# Mean Girls Rule

Everyone wanted a piece of the brand new, 1912, U. Penn grad, Dr. Alice Paul; she just wanted to be Alice, and more and more she saw herself as a spokeswoman with a mission. Though her doctorate should naturally lead to a career in academia, Alice's experiences and Quaker heritage led her elsewhere. Teaching was the one career clearly open to women, but in a pithy letter to her old Swarthmore pal, Mabel Vernon, she wrote, "There are plenty of people to teach school."[34]

Offers abounded. Alice was famous now due to her demonstrated effectiveness as an organizer and a fund raiser. Her old buddy from Phillie, Jane Campbell, was anxious to repeat their successful actions of summer, 1911, especially since the annual NAWSA convention would be held in Philadelphia. A grand parade would be a splendid way to welcome the delegates, though floats were prohibited. Alice, having cut her teeth on the Pankhursts' spectacles, couldn't imagine a low key parade, and for Alice, a parade without floats was a cake with no icing.

They wanted Alice in Ohio and in New York Harriot Blatch (daughter of Elizabeth Cady Stanton) offered her a paying job. She might have been tempted

---

[34] Suffragist: AP to Vernon, 21 April 1913, Reel 2

---

81

because up there in New York City, Harriot Blatch's annual parade was causing an annual uproar. It had all begun in 1910 when Harriot was frustrated and hoppin' mad at the New York State Legislators' continued refusal to consider a suffrage measure. "Mankind is moved to action by emotion, not by argument and reason," she announced. And so she proclaimed that what "could be more stirring than hundreds of women, carrying banners, marching -----marching------!" [35] By 1912 about 10,000 people had taken to the streets and marched from Washington Square all along Fifth Avenue, cheered on and acclaimed by sidewalks jammed with spectators. New York suffrage would happen...though it remained five years away.

Now that was the kind of action that Alice had in mind. She had a vision and she immediately set about putting it in place. Her love life was secondary to her mission as her faithful admirer William Parker was soon to learn. Intimate dinner dates, warm correspondence, was the best she could do for now. William's continued devotion was delightful, but blatant insults to women infuriated her. William and love were on hold till she was done with this suffrage issue. That shouldn't take long. Her cause was so right, she had only to make it happen.

## Basic Differences and the Catt Fight Begins

Currently, the suffragist thrust was aimed at an orderly, state by state, enfranchisement for women. That plan wasn't working very well for a variety of reasons, but mostly having to do with the obstruction

---

[35] Blatch, Harriot Stanton and Lutz, Alma *Challenging Years*, (Westport, Connecticut: Hyperion Press, 1940), 129

coming from state legislators. In one case the constitutional amendment had to first be passed by the state's two legislative chambers, and then subjected to a referendum. Slim chance of passage, all the legislators and referendum voters were men.

Alice did the math. In 1912 nine states, western all, had granted votes for women: Wyoming 1890, Colorado 1893, Utah & Idaho 1896, Washington & California 1911, Oregon, Kansas, & Arizona 1912. With 48 states in the union, NASWA needed approval from the current 39 remaining states, whose southern and eastern contingencies were generally, adamantly opposed.

If the Anthony Amendment passed the U.S. Congress, it would have to be ratified by a 3/4 majority, that was 36 states, a better chance than the excruciating, one-by-one, process advocated by NASWA, improbably passed in what was predictable and probable southern opposition.

Since Alice viewed the cause through a different lens, she set about enacting her plan for a constitutional amendment with her characteristic, unfettered vision. The women's outright and determined demand that the rights of citizens of the United States to vote shall not be denied or abridged by the United States or any state on account of sex, is hardly a shocking notion in the 21st century, but a gob-smacker in the views of the 20th, and absurdly apparent to Alice's Quaker informed mind.

But what was obvious to Alice, escaped the minds of many prominent suffragists, since for some, such a notion smacked of militancy. To these same women, Alice's association with the Pankhursts would forever make her suspect, a sort of bad girl. Others simply felt it an impossible and foolish endeavor. The NASWA leaders continued the annual charade of presenting the Anthony Amendment to committees of both the House and the Senate. Small wonder that Alice's support for the amendment was considered futile.

Harriot Blatch turned down Alice Paul's request for support, responding that she thought a national campaign premature. Her plan was to first obtain the vote for women in a large eastern state, namely New York. However, Harriot did the next best thing. She introduced Alice to Jane Addams, the internationally renowned founder of Chicago's Hull House and NASWA's vice-president. Addams had her own agenda, votes for women would empower those most opposed to the political influence of the greedy corporate barons currently causing horrendous working and living conditions.

Addams immediately suggested that Alice be appointed to the National's Congressional Committee (CC), a sow's ear of a committee but the only one involved in a Federal initiative. The CC's task was to engage in that useless annual presentation of the Anthony Amendment to the congress. Its prior chair had received a yearly budget of $10. When that nice lady resigned, she returned change from the ten.

Yet more good news, Lucy Burns was home for good. Reluctantly the board appointed Alice, chair of the CC, and her fellow Pankhurst Untouchable Lucy, as second. Then they should just go away and bang their silly heads against the legislation's wall. But they should first move to Washington. And they should pay their own way, support themselves, and raise their own operating funds.

Alice's eyes danced in anticipation. Finally, she was in charge of her very own campaign, and she knew exactly where that was going. Big time! A super parade, down Pennsylvania Avenue, with bands and floats and banners and hilarious support for women's votes.   It was all in her head. Now there was only the doing of it.

Immediately Alice shipped out for DC and the rest is history.

# Chapter 13
# Crunch Time, *But Suppose You Gave a Parade and Nobody Came !*

Alice arrived in Washington in December, with visions of marchers dancing in her head. No cozy armchairs, roaring fires and family gatherings at Paulsdale for her this Christmas. It was December 7, 1912 and there was absolutely no time to waste. No matter that her accommodations were Spartan, she and Lucy had figured they'd have the women's suffrage amendment passed in Congress by year's end, an ambitious goal. In later life she chuckled at her naiveté. [36]

Since she had less than three months to organize the first, the most spectacular women's march in Washington's history, Alice shifted into crisis mode. NAWSA had furnished her with a list of over forty possible supporters. "…, I began on the list, maybe alphabetically as they gave it to me. …But I found one person after another after another had died, and then I found one after another after another after another had moved away and nobody knew their present address. …[37] The list was useless.

---

[36] Zahniser, p.126

[37] *Conversations with Alice Paul*, 64

Alice was now all alone, friendless and without hope, Lucy, done for good with England, was back in Brooklyn, luxuriating in the warmth of a family Christmas. She would not arrive till middle –January. NASWA' s support was not only bogus but, reflecting their sentiments, haughty and obnoxious about not supplying one penny to the Congressional Committee. Alice ruefully realized she, little Alice, had almost no time to pull off an earthshaking and largely unwelcome event.

In fact, given her odds, any sane person would just quit. But Alice was scared, not down, and she was single minded and resourceful. Like mining little gems, Alice was able to ferret out suffragist sympathizers from the conservative ranks she faced. She kept hearing that no one was interested in suffrage "because this was a Congressional and Diplomatic City…that parades, open air speakers or demonstrations of any kind would alienate the few who were interested… .[38] She called on the indomitable spirit of her Quaker ancestors and with only a few other prospects, she reluctantly turned to her CC predecessor, Elizabeth Kent. But she wasn't expecting much. Anybody who had change from a ten-dollar budget most likely wasn't very active. She was in for a shock. "Mrs. William Kent asked me to have Christmas dinner with them …. She was the most stalwart and wonderful aide anyone could ever want, my predecessor, Extra, extra, extra, *extra* wonderful." [39] Alice could be generous with her praise

---

38 Zahniser & Fr, p.127

39 *Conversations with Alice Paul*, p.63

---

Now she would get on with her task. Her defunct little Congressional Committee began to thrive on the oxygen Alice put out and donations began to arrive with amazing speed. Emma Gillett, one of only four practicing female lawyers in town, volunteered as treasurer and found an office. It was cold and dark, situated below street level but it lent an air of credibility to the fledgling cause. Then Santa arrived in the person of Elizabeth Kent who would gift the cause with $5 monthly to help defray the sixty-dollar rent.

Alice relegated herself to the basement and could be seen, wearing a rakish purple hat, and warming her hands in a furry muff. She was there all day making calls, recruiting contacts and suffrage groups, and raising money. Though Alice had a glorious vision for her parade she feared that marchers could be few since she learned that many educated and wealthy women found such a display unseemly.

Well she'd dazzle her audience with footwork, she'd offer up a feast of eye candy loaded with banners, bands, floats, chariots, assorted marchers of every age and ethnicity sporting capes of the purple, white and green colors of a suffragist. Commanding all eyes, astride a tall white stallion, the "Suffrage Herald" beautiful, bold Inez Mulholland would sweep down the avenue, heralding the "New Woman." She'd command the scene with splendor, and on the evening of the new U.S. president's inauguration, a clear message of a woman's right to vote would be proclaimed to the whole world.

Alice had it all in her mind. Enthusiasm grew. Curiosity seekers and volunteers jammed the little office on F Street. Typewriters clacked, pins, pamphlets, posters were sold. All was well, and then, sadly, Alice found herself playing Whack-a-Mole with problems.

Not the last problem, but a potential parade killer surfaced. Alice wanted Pennsylvania Avenue and she would have it on March 3rd the day before the inauguration. But the entrenched prejudice of so many Washingtonians did not confine itself to African-Americans bias. There was plenty of animosity left over for women and their "frivolous" causes.

## A Women's Parade? Ridiculous!

Shortly after her arrival in December, Alice had approached Police Commissioner Richard Sylvester. Looking up at his prodigious bulk, she politely requested a permit for a parade. Furthermore, she would like to schedule it on March 3rd and use Pennsylvania Avenue. He said "No," but suggested March 5th down 16th Street. He gave his reasons. So many men, southern Democrats in town to celebrate, would party in saloons. He assumed that these same drunks would harass the women marchers. Also he had a small police force that would be stretched for duty two consecutive days and on March 5th the suffragists would be free to use 16th Street, a prettier street, away from the crowds with little need for protection. Now she should go away.

Alice said, "No."

She would not be put off. Many women, potential suffragists, would be accompanying their fathers and husbands, arriving early for the inauguration, an audience she wanted to reach. Also, if men could march on Pennsylvania Avenue, women could too.

Sylvester said, "No."

89

For weeks Alice persisted, bringing prominent women, the wives and daughters of congressmen, with her to his office. She badgered him with supporting civic organizations, the Chamber of Commerce, the Merchants Association and other strident voices.

Finally, Sylvester said, "Okay, you can have March 3$^{rd}$, but no Pennsylvania Avenue."

So then she went over his head, to his boss, Commissioner John A. Johnston. He was even more dismissive, vaguely suggesting "another time in another place." But he did pass the buck to the Inauguration Chairman, William Eustis, he figured a sure fire refusal, no fan of the suffragists.

So all was lost and gloom prevailed. It was the first week in January and the women despaired. Their parade would have to happen on 16$^{th}$ street and nobody would come. Doughty Alice just dug in. "Miss Paul would not give up on the Avenue. None of us wanted to but she had the courage to go on."[40] Suddenly, to the women's amazement, for reasons they could only guess, Chairman Eustis said, "Yes." The women could have their parade on Pennsylvania Avenue and they could hold it on March 3$^{rd.}$ .

With the time and place now determined. Alice and friends would create a most colossal spectacle. On the day before the inauguration of the president they hadn't elected, they would march in glory down Pennsylvania Avenue, pass a planned pageant on the Treasury steps, and on past the White House to a

[40] Paul to Rheta Childe Dorr, 22 February, 1914 National Women's Party Papers

jubilant rally on 17th Street. And they had a little over seven weeks to put this miracle together.

Some minor issues emerged, NASWA ever irksome, resented the traditional tricolors Alice proposed as too reminiscent of those brazen British suffragettes. Easily solved, Alice ordered up sashes of their blue and yellow colors.

## Alice Confronts Racism

But it got harder. Alice's plan for parade participants would be diverse; votes for women for Alice meant all women. She was a Quaker whose faith emphasized equality for all, in theory, and though not without its own bigotry, her New Jersey upbringing had not prepared her for the extent of virulent racism in 1913 Washington. Advisors warned her of attitudes, and Alice had to wrestle with the threat of white participants refusing to march alongside the black suffragists. Additionally, there would be a large influx of notoriously bigoted southerners in Washington to support Virginian Woodrow Wilson.

Alice so feared failure that she decided not to actively solicit the burgeoning black women's movement. At this point a parade was imminent and she felt its success crucial to suffrage. Under the current circumstances she even considered excluding the black women because practically speaking she felt "Our winning the suffrage will be the thing that will most raise the status of negro women as well as white women." She would simply ignore the issue in hopes that it would just go away.

But African American women wouldn't just go away. Then Alice wondered why they should? Their voices had equal rights to be heard. Two groups from

Howard University applied for march assignments and Alice, obeying her better instincts, said yes. They would be included with other colleges in the same section in which she and Lucy Burns would march. End of discussion. Rich white ladies should suffer.

That settled, Alice could turn her attention to raising the desperately needed cash for the floats, the bands, banners, costumes and office rent. Expenses were mounting and since there was no "Deep Pockets" who would sponsor such a questionable event, Alice shifted into merchandizing mode. All sorts of items were for sale, but the most lucrative was the deal Alice struck with Wilson's inaugural committee. She persuaded the Treasury Department to build grandstands for the pageant she'd planned to be held on their Treasury Building's steps, benches which could also be used for the next day's inaugural parade. Then she sold the seats and netted $2,000., a healthy bit of change but only a small part of the $14,000 in ultimate parade expenses. Frenzied days flew by and March 3 arrived.

But Alice and Lucy gasped... what if they gave a big parade and nobody came!

# Chapter 14
# March Madness

"Nobody ever dreamt that women-you were always seeing these Elks and people going around in processions-but they never thought of women doing such a thing. And so there really was a great interest in it. A great many tickets were being sold, to our astonishment, so when the day came, almost time for the procession we found that apparently the police were taking the matter very casually. They said, 'Well maybe a handful of police could tend to it on the day before the inaugural.' And that they would concentrate all their force on taking care of the people at the inaugural." [44] Police Commissioner Sylvester had always wished that Alice and her silly suffragists would just go away.

Alice knew his kind and so on the night before the march, Mrs. Rogers, a committee member. "... said she would take me down...and talk to her brother-in-law, [Secretary of War Henry Lewis Stimson] to see if he couldn't be aroused into the fact that we really were in some doubt as to whether the police could handle the

93

crowds…"[41] Canny Alice always realized the power of connections, and wasn't surprised when Stimson assured the ladies that his cavalry was a phone call away. "I'll send over the cavalry. They will handle everything you need."[42]

So everything was in place on a sunny March 3rd afternoon. The fabulous spectacle had been well planned and all were poised to march. Crisp winds fanned the ebullient women and those few men who supported them. Suffragist groups from all over America had sent delegations and waited on side streets for the starting signal. Workers, farmers, homemakers, doctors, actresses, librarians, collegians in gowns, women, grouped by profession and dressed in colorful garb stood at the ready. Exhausted suffragist "Pilgrims" having walked for three weeks, 200 miles from Newark, New Jersey," waited in bedraggled formation. Parade Floats, twenty in number, would be piped along by the nine bands now sending discordant notes as they warmed their brass. The four mounted brigades' horses pawed the pavement impatient to command attention. Inez Milholland, resplendent in a white suit and deep blue cape, struggling to restrain "Grey Dawn" her feisty stallion, would lead the march with awesome majesty.

And so, at 3:25 the starting gun sounded and the parade commenced with a triumphant roar. The leading contingent proudly stepped off down Pennsylvania Avenue, so proud, so righteous, so blissfully unaware of the boiling hot, hate-filled men and boys lining the streets.

---

[41] *Conversations with Alice Paul*, p.71

[42] Ibid 72

Then it happened.  After just three short blocks, the crowds broke through the police barriers and surged onto the street so as to make it impossible for the marchers to move ahead. A line of four women became three, then two, then one solitary suffragist struggling to trudge ahead.

The women were taunted, grabbed, shoved and ridiculed.  Instead of protecting the women, the police seemed to enjoy all the ribald jokes and laughter and in part, participated in them. One policeman explained that they should stay at home where they belonged if they didn't want trouble.  …Two ambulances came and went constantly for six hours, always impeded and at times actually opposed, so the doctor and driver literally had to fight their way to give succor to the injured."[43]

"Further back in the procession…Men snatched banners, tugged at women's clothing and sometimes the women themselves, and tried to climb the floats. They hurled lighted cigarettes and matches, and reached out their canes to dislodge women's hats, pinched and spit and shouted insults…even more shocking to the women was the conduct of their protectors…"[46]

Alice was no stranger to mob violence. Against ridiculous odds, she and others, fought back against the angry surging tide. These women and those few men, determined suffragists sympathizers all, had come too far to be defeated now.  Women linked arms and pushed ahead. At the front, Inez Milholland, rode Grey Dawn dead ahead into the crowds, scattering them as she carried on with her task to lead.

---

[43] Library of Congress, American Memory, Harvey, Sheridan: *Marching for the Vote: Remembering the Woman Suffrage Parade of 1913* [46] Walton, p. 75

---

95

Alice and Lucy commandeered a car and likewise provided a wedge into the mob. Still dressed in the gown she was to wear as a member of the college contingent, and ever the activist, Alice jumped from the car and proceeded to clear obstructers with outstretched arms.

Even a Boy Scout troop pitched in; they had been commissioned to ward off mice toting pranksters. These 400 boy sympathizers, wielding batons, outdid the police in checking the crowds. But the score was still Crowds 1, Suffragists 0.

Meanwhile, back at the train station, newly elected President Wilson arrived for his next day's inauguration anticipating the adoring crowds of supporters who weren't there, since over a half-million people had assembled at the Suffragist Parade. History has him wondering where his crowds were, only to find he'd been upstaged by those very women he would grow to detest.

Police Commissioner Sylvester, attending the president, suddenly got nervous at the reports of dangerous mayhem on Pennsylvania Avenue, and the failure of his own force to prevent disaster on the parade route. Reluctantly, he placed the phone call that brought the local cavalry swooping down on the raucous melee. Ignoring the Washington police, the cavalry took command and charged into the crowds, scattering the mob and forcing a retreat.

So hours later, with order largely restored, the parade resumed. Ida Wells-Barnett, ignoring the NASWA's segregation order, took her rightful place with the all-white Illinois delegation. The Pilgrims, gathered in their tattered long brown capes, even drew cheers from the newly subdued bystanders. The featured tableau resumed on the Treasury Building steps. In filmy gauze costumes, women symbols of Justice, Charity, Hope and Liberty performed an exuberant dance before "Colombia," joyously celebrating the arrival of the new woman, virtuous and strong and hopefully, soon to be enfranchised.

The gala post parade rally at DAR Continental Hall, planned to celebrate a crowning achievement became a constant gripe fest. NASWA leader Anna Howard Shaw lashed out in her address. "Never was I so ashamed of our national capital before. If anything could prove the need of the ballot, nothing could prove it more that the treatment we received today." [44] She demanded an investigation of the performance of Police Commissioner Sylvester. They'd have his head!

Alice looked at the parade fiasco through a different lens. They carped; she schemed. Back in the F Street office, that very day, Alice seized the moment. Surrounded by the remnants of the parade paraphernalia, hatless, still wearing her academic gown she immediately swung into action. She knew that the deliberate neglect at the hands of the police was probably the best thing that ever happened to the movement.

The public would sympathize with the mistreated women and her cause for a constitutional amendment would be greatly enhanced. Lemonade!

---

[44] Zanheiser & Fry, p.149

## *Lagniappe: 2017 The Mother of all Marches*

Woodrow Wilson lamented the lack of numbers present at his arrival on inauguration eve, March 3, 1913. Mostly the anticipated crowd was elsewhere, attending Alice Paul's first ever 1913 Women's March. History repeated itself when yet another U.S. president, Donald Trump on January 21[st,] 2017, a day after his inauguration. was treated to the spectacle of an outpouring of women in the largest one-day march in American history, *The Women's March on Washington.* (See book cover)

President Trump might have been dismayed also, as the number of marchers, estimated at about 500,000, was possibly greater than the audience at his inauguration. And that his estimated 300,000 to 500,000 turnout was in DC.

Around the nation and across the globe, women, and many men too, took to the streets to demonstrate. Banners, posters, bright pink hats (see book cover) sent their messages from towns and cities all the way from frigid Fairbanks to sunny California. Worldwide, millions of women marched in 261 locations ranging from Antarctica to Zimbabwe.

Women were united and mad. They had many issues to address, essentially women's issues but also racial and gender equality, immigration reform and pressing environmental concerns. Though the spectacle of millions of women around the world was astounding, what of the 2017 march? Was it one & done or, in effect, a turning point in women's history? Would the enthusiasm that powered the marches the following year, in 2018, presage an annual event? For sure, it inspired large numbers of women to run for office, and the "Power to the Polls" rallies urged women to register and vote.

The Women's March lives now as an annual January event. Check out Womansmarch.com. or find a march near you at www.womensmarch.com

# Part Four: The Wheels Grind
# (March 4, 1913-April 6, 1917)
## Chapter 15
## First Catt Fight

Alice knew a gift when she saw one. Lessons taught by the Pankhursts applied here: use adverse publicity generated by loutish behavior to energize your people and to advance your cause. Likewise, the national newspapers knew red meat when it was served. Several framed the men's behavior as a typical "boys will be boys" response to loose women. A San Francisco journalist claimed "Not a single man among the thousands of spectators thought of votes for women." The Washington Post, which just didn't get it, jubilantly stated "Miles of Fluttering Femininity Present Entrancing Suffrage Appeal." Sexist Post editors, focusing on the women, entirely missed the point of the parade.

But a journalistic belief in freedom of speech did forge a grudging acknowledgement of the women's bravery and determination, and Alice's parade put suffragists exactly where she had planned. Now they could be cast in the role of righteous, respectable women who had been victimized for their beliefs.

Those few sympathetic congressmen who had marched in the parade were likewise infuriated at the women's ill treatment by both the spectators and the police. On the following day, just before the inauguration, these outraged politicians scheduled quick sessions in both the House and the Senate chambers. "The House minority leader, James Mann

(Republican, IL) aroused even more anger by suggesting that one put-upon woman, 'ought to have been at home.' 'She had as much right there as any one,' shouted marcher John Raker (Democrat, CA). A resolution resulted. An investigation would probe the parade's injustices and affirm the women's rights to "parade freely and unmolested." Commissioner Sylvester would eventually be fired.

The attention brought to the suffragists also unearthed the hydra-headed monster they faced, and opposition emerged to the cause from anti suffragists for a variety of reasons. Some feared the participation of "inferior races" a code name for black women and immigrants. Liquor interests feared that a vote for women would mean prohibition of the sale of alcohol. Many women equated women's rights demonstrations with militancy of the Pankhurst type…dreadful and probably socialist too. Their vision of women was so elevated that in their minds, women, the more virtuous human beings, should use their superior moral authority to counsel men and therefore, not need to vote at all.

Some friends just viewed the matter differently, advocating for state-by-state approval. Alice's supporter Harriot Blatch felt that if a large state like her New York caved, others would quickly follow. Her supporter Elizabeth Rogers wrote to Alice in no uncertain terms, "The constitutional amendment business at this stage of the game is such nonsense."[48] For Alice, friends like this made enemies unnecessary.

And then there were the legislative challenges. Passage of a constitutional amendment requires a two-thirds majority vote in both the House and the Senate and if so, the amendment must then be ratified by three-fourths of the states. Alice could derive some certain encouragement by the recent passage of the Sixteenth and Seventeenth Amendments, which guaranteed income tax and the popular election of senators, respectively. At least Congress was moving on some selected issues.

But post parade, Alice never let up. Two more deputations to the White House failed to impress the president, but they did manage to unnerve the national. Shaw and Catt ever uneasy about the Paul and Burns' Pankhurst connection, shrunk from the use of any action which might be construed as militant. Word of the CC's activities reached Dr. Shaw and she summoned Alice and Lucy to her home in Moylan, Pennsylvania. But to Shaw's dismay, the girls made nice during the visit, then went home and stirred the pot again. And furthermore, they didn't ask Dr. Boss Lady's permission. Though the national gave her cover, Alice was here; they were there. Alice wanted more control over her finances and her agenda, and so her NAWSA Congressional Committee gave birth to the Congressional Union, the naughty CU, the orphan step-child of an orphan step-child. But the birth of this rebel babe would be painful, a prolonged and difficult labor. That move made Dr. Shaw nervous, who feared those young, upstarts would attract both money and members away from the national. She sent Dora Lewis to inform Alice that the CU was to have no association with them, the National, financial or otherwise. Bad enough, but then this new CU thing, announced that it planned to start its own weekly newspaper, the *Suffragist*. It would be dedicated to keeping their cause in front of the public, and advocating for the passage of a suffragist amendment. Its editor would be Rheta

Childe Dorr, a close associate of the dreaded Pankhursts, whom Alice and Lucy still refused to vilify.

Then, much to Dr. Shaw's distress., the first edition of *The Suffragist* featured a smirking caricature of Woodrow Wilson. The comical portrayal of the president, Shaw said, "Made me sick at heart."[45] Alice and Lucy agreed that the cover was unfortunate, but argued that they hadn't seen it before publication.

### Alice Attacks

When the Senate Committee on Woman Suffrage issued a favorable report in June, 1913, Alice responded immediately with the announcement of yet another demonstration. On July 31, Alice was in Hyattsville, Maryland, to greet delegates from all over the nation gathered for a mass rally. This time many did not arrive on foot, or train. They drove. Drove? Hundreds of women drove themselves from states up and down the east coast, modern women making a statement in the most modern of inventions.

The following day their motorcade descended on Washington, other delegates walking the six miles behind them. This time they were scrupulously protected by DC police. A chastised Commissioner Sylvester had mustered a considerable force. There'd be no mayhem at this parade. The women and some supportive senators were escorted to the Senate Chamber where they delivered petitions bearing 80,000 signatures and listened to 21 senators speak in favor of the suffragist amendment. Alice seated in the great hall, thrilled with pride; so much support had to mean a constitutional amendment could not be far away. Alice was so wrong.

---

[45] Walton, p.88.

Across the pond, in England Emmaline Pankhurst's suffragettes, more and more frustrated with their lack of progress, were increasingly militant. When Emmaline and her crew set off a bomb at the home of Prime Minister Lloyd George, she was jailed. The police accustomed now to the suffragette hunger strikes and being condemned for their forced feedings, had developed a new policy. The striker would be released until she recovered, then incarcerated again. Emmaline, sentenced to three years in prison, must have played with the numbers because in the fall of 1913 she arrived in America for a cross country fundraising tour. Alice and Lucy welcomed and assisted their former mentor, further irritating Anna Shaw and the "ladylike" gang at NASWA.

During the preceding summer the CU/National relationship had deteriorated, its love/hate balance turning sour. Alice and Lucy acted and organized in their own way, recruiting and fund raising and speaking as they willed. But since they were still affiliated with the NASWA, their behavior could be seen as a reflection of the National's policies.

When Lucy was arrested for chalking a sidewalk, she ventured, "In New York and other cities writing on the sidewalk is not prohibited. [46] But to some it smacked of militancy. Lucy paid the $1.00 fine and laughed, labeling chalking sidewalks simply as an economical form of advertising. Neither Anna Howard Shaw or Carrie Chapman Catt would ever stoop to writing on a sidewalk and Lucy was apprised of her transgression. "You may think we are a set of old fogies, and perhaps we are, for I think there are certain

[46] Walton, p.89.

laws of order which should be followed by everyone."
She went on " It requires a good deal more courage to
work steadily and steadfastly for forty or fifty years to
gain an end than it does to do a[n] impulsive rash thing
and lose it."[47] Lucy replied respectively to the older
women. Always witty, she pointed out that they'd
garnered a week of public advertising for a mere dollar
bill.

But with the scent of militancy detectable, it
probably didn't help matters that their good friend
Emmaline arrived in Washington the following week as
the guest of Alice and Lucy. The annual NASAW
Convention was to begin shortly thereafter, in
November. With such questionable behavior, and
obvious faults, Dr. Shaw and C.C. Catt could hardly
tolerate the CU's dynamic duo. They'd need to be
destroyed and the convention would provide just the
opportunity.

## Splitsville

Alice harbored no confusions about her agenda.
The CU was a one-trick-horse-and-pony show focused
on a congressional amendment insuring votes for
women. Not everyone loved Alice's ideas.

In her interview with Alice, Amelia Fry asked,
"During that period, in 1913, were you aware that the
National American officers, like Dr. Shaw and so forth,
did not want all this effort put out for a national
amendment, that they wanted more state-by–state
campaigns?

Paul: Mrs. Stanley McCormick and Mrs. [Carrie
Chapman] Catt made a protest at the convention against

---

[47] Zahneiser & Fry, p.175.

what we were doing, which is the first time that I realized it. Perhaps it was dumb not to realize it before, but I didn't."[48]

Unwittingly, Alice's report on the activities of the CU infuriated the already angry trio of Shaw, Catt and McCormick. "...and so I made the report, saying we had this big procession and we had had so many similar processions, and we'd had so many deputations to the President, and we raised so much money, which I think was $27,000, if I remember rightly, not very much but still a lot for us, and we started a weekly paper..."[49]

Alice stepped down, proud, smiling, anticipating overwhelming approval for her valuable contributions to the suffrage cause, blithely unaware of the fact that she had just dug her own grave. Ironically, with no fun intended, Mrs. Catt used the analogy of the CU as a dog's tail wagging its body. Then McCormick, the treasurer piled on, declaring the not one penny of the $27,000 raised had been handed over to the National's treasury. She declared that it was intolerable that one committee could raise all that money, and keep it.

Everyone knew which committee had done just that. It took the highly respected board member Jane Addams to remind Mrs. McCormick that "NAWSA had *insisted* that the Congressional Committee raise its own operating funds, and that NAWSA had further made it clear that no financial help would be forthcoming from the national treasury."[50] Furthermore, she had carefully

---

[48] Conversations with Alice Paul, p. 86

[49] Ibid, 87

[50] Ibid.88

examined Alice's financial report and found it impeccable. Alice and Lucy and the CU had all the momentum.

National's leadership viewed that as a threat. Wisdom might have prodded the National with the old adage, if you can't beat it, join it, but Catt seemed to have had her own reasons for resenting Alice. Twenty years prior to the convention she was young and ambitious too. Full of enthusiasm she'd organized a committee and raised funds to get some life into a staid NASWA. But her vision was squashed by the old guard members and she acquiesced. It wasn't fair that now Alice wouldn't cave to her. The Cattfight would dog Alice thereafter. Catt's animosity would only grow with time.

Anna Shaw had her own set of demons. Though brilliant and accomplished, she was a mediocre administrator of the National, and was always looking over her shoulder at Carrie Catt. Now she had the upstart CU to contend with, and furthermore, Alice Paul and Lucy Burns distinctly smelled like Pankhursts.

Up until now Alice assumed that she was okay. She was even proud of her considerable accomplishments. The animosity generated by the National's leaders stunned her and she dropped out to rest and recover her purpose. Lucy alone answered the leaders' summit to New York, for their effort to resolve the differences. Dr. Shaw had a great idea. She would start a whole new Congressional Committee and Lucy could be the chair, Alice could come along too, as a member. Somehow Lucy was able to reject this offer, so Shaw decided to form a whole new CC and placed another woman named McCormick in charge. She was Ruth Hanna McCormick and the operative word here

107

was "Hanna." Mrs. Medill McCormick was the daughter of Mark Hanna, one of the most powerful political bosses of the Republican Party.

McCormick was surrounded by her father's operatives who convinced her that "if you look over the world there was almost no place where women could vote…and they convinced her it was an impossible thing to take a great nation like the United States and go out of step with the rest of the world."[51] They would advocate in Congress for a bill mandating each state to place on the ballot, a referendum on suffrage, the Shafroth-Palmer Bill.

Alice wondered about the efficacy of a state-by-state referendum on which only men would vote. In despair their little CU group gathered, fully aware of the imbalance of power they confronted. They would make their case to the National for a constitutional amendment, the Anthony Amendment. Their first clue that they wouldn't prevail was that the treasurer, Mrs. Stanley McCormick took her chair and turned it so that her back was to the group. She remained so for the entire meeting.

Back home "So we seriously considered whether we hadn't better just give it up and disband and go home and let them go ahead and do the best they could. But we finally, all of us, agreed that…we'd better turn in and try to make another organization, because then we were only an affiliate … I think they came to the same conclusion."[52]

---

[51] Ibid, 91
[52] Conversations with Alice Paul, 92

National came up with a contrived solution whereby the CU could become yet another completely separate organization. Discouraged now, Alice applied for their new organization. "They accepted our resignation but didn't accept our application for the new one."

Alice and Lucy knew then that they were terminated by National. Nervous and with mixed feelings they determined not to quit but instead to create a brave new entity, it would be given the title of the Congressional Union for Women's Suffrage. The good news then was that they were now entirely independent; the bad news was they were now entirely independent.

On January 11, 1914 Mrs. Elizabeth Kent entertained 400 of the CU's supporters in her spacious home. Alice and Lucy, could rely on their indomitable inner strength, but had to wonder about their own people's resolve under NASWA's pressure. To their delight, no member of their old committee defected. "every single person of the old congressional committee stood with us."

The road to success suddenly looked less rocky; Alice Paul was born into Quaker values.  Her celebration of these Quaker precepts, and her coming of age with the Pankhursts produced the rock hard, independent visionary she became post National. Free now to follow her own instincts, she'd come too far for further distractions. It was dead speed ahead for Alice. NASWA be damned.

The new CU was hardly democratic, a feature which Dr. Shaw wasted no time in remarking. Though Alice's sole purpose was equal rights for women, she was expedient. She didn't feature endless discussions prior to decisions, an aspect of the National that Alice wanted to avoid. She would move quickly in response to situations. She lost some disgruntled members, but gained some admirers such as Alva Vanderbuilt Belmont whose name says it all and Katherine Hepburn, whose name is not quiet either.

But having expelled the CU and its collection of rowdies, NASWA wasn't finished. Most likely counseled by her father, McCormick, countered with a devastating tactic. In a frontal blow to Alice's constitutional amendment initiative, they proposed the Shafroth-Palmer Amendment, a regurgitation of their State-by-State process towards suffrage. It was proposed that in any state where there was an eight percent approval gained by petition, a referendum for women's vote would be placed upon the ballot.

In May, McCormick approached Alice for permission to take part in a CU Suffrage Parade. Naïve Alice, learned too late that wily Mrs. McCormick had entered a float showcasing her Shafroth-Palmer Amendment. So the CU parade actually advertised McCormick's initiative. Later Alice laughed it off; "Well, most of the people that looked on had no idea what was the Shafroth-Palmer."

Then, to further embarrass the CU, the National spoke urgently for a Senate vote on the Anthony Amendment, knowing well it would be defeated and Alice would be humiliated. The vote was held. They were right; Boss Hanna knew how to operate.

In June, the *Suffragist* Editor, Rheta Childe Dorr, brought 500 club women to a meeting with

President Wilson. As usual, the President feigned helplessness. The power lay in the congress, he averred, indeed a true statement, though he could influence his party's votes. He continued to claim that only a state-by-state, creeping approval would work. A southerner himself, he had to know southern congressmen were already busy repressing the black man's vote and wouldn't care to add black women's suffrage. Wilson grew agitated at the prospect of an amendment and by August, votes for women was a dead issue in Congress.

Maybe the mayhem of 1914 was affecting the President's good humor. The European war that so many foresaw arrived with the assassination of heir to the Austro Hungarian throne, Archduke Ferdinand. Wilson wrestled with the potential future involvement of the U.S. in a foreign war. Was there be a role for America in that conflict? Then there was another calamity, much closer to home. The First Lady, Ellen Wilson, mother of their three daughters, died in August, 1914, from kidney disease. The bereaved president managed to rally though, in 1915 he married Edith Galt, heir to the jewelry store fortune, and finally quieted the salty gossip around their relationship.

### Alice Plays a New Game ... Power Politics

Alice had another idea. Wilson's insistence on the case for suffrage laying in the hands of the Congress, in this case the Democrats, inspired her plot. She would hold the party in power, the Democrats, responsible for passing the constitutional amendment. She would manage to bring pressure to bear on these men to move forward on the Anthony Amendment. No matter that she would also have to campaign against those senators who had supported her.

Fortunately, her well-heeled cohort, Alva Belmont agreed and invited the newly formed CU Advisory Council to Marble House, her "Cottage" located on Millionaire's Row, the parade of mansions defining extravagance along the seaside in Newport, Rhode Island. The women had to be encouraged in their mission by remarking that the façade of the fabulous Marble House, was similar to the President's White House. Alice, the frugal Quaker, recognized the relationship of money to political access and gratefully accepted Alva's $5,000. donation to her initiative.

"We called this meeting... I presided at the meeting and gave the outline of what we wanted to do. And Lucy Burns, who had been doing most of the congressional work, made the *splendid* speech showing how the Democrats had caucused against us as a whole body, and we couldn't start and support individual Democratic candidates even though they were for us, when they belonged to a caucus that had taken action against us...so this vote went unanimously through."[53]

Alice thought she had made it clear from the beginning...suffrage was a political issue. The political party in power could make it happen, no matter if it was Republican or Democrat. The dominant party could pass her congressional amendment, now officially, the Anthony Amendment. That to the simply determined Alice was clearly a non-partisan statement. So, she would send women out west to those states which

---

[53] Conversations with Alice Paul, p. 108.

---

allowed women to vote. Her emissaries were sent forth with instructions to campaign against the Democrat candidate, a counter intuitive command to many and source of derision from Shaw and McCormick.

Because Alice never spared herself, she had no problem asking others to do likewise. She had to know that the women she sent west were stepping into hell, a problematic non-starter in her mind. Seven women, (later twelve) would revel in a grand send off and board a special train car in Union Station heading west. They would travel together to Chicago, then separate into twosomes, take on their daunting tasks in the individual states to which they were assigned. California, Colorado, Kansas, Oregon, Washington, Nevada, Idaho, Wyoming, and Arizona, all suffrage states were the targets.

But the merry band departed Washington in September with just one month to work miracles. Alice supplied them well with the tools of persuasion, she packed posters, and flyers, and copies of the *Suffragist*. Stuffed in their travelling kits were the CU banners, the purple, white and yellow drapes would adorn the fronts of the headquarters they were to set up immediately upon arrival at their assigned cities. And they were to raise money too.

If these women thought they would be well received, they must have been sadly disappointed. Only Lucy and Rose Winslow, a Polish emigre, in California were roundly supported. The others' receptions ranged from support, to yawns, to hostility. Many saw these women as interlopers, interfering in their states' politics. They couldn't be too surprised that those

Democrat congressmen who had supported the suffrage cause fiercely resented CU's support for their Republican opponents.

Alice, in Washington, had her own set of problems. She was confronted with empty coffers and demands for money from her women on the front lines, in response, she spent day and night fundraising. Then there was the Pankhurst effect, i.e. the pernicious perception that women's activism was militancy in skirts. In 1914 it was never in good taste for a woman to raise her voice. Doing so on a street corner was unthinkable. Though Emmaline & Co. had temporarily eschewed their harassment of English parliamentarians, and turned their concerted attention to the war effort, right minded Americans still feared outspoken women.

In November the voters' scores were tallied. Despite the fact that most of the opposed Democrat candidates were reelected, Alice declared victory. The suffragist cause had emerged from the darkness and was now elevated to a major role in their campaigns. The party in power should take note. Though two states, Nevada and Montana, were added to the women's voter list, five states, North and South Dakota, Nebraska, Montana, and Ohio turned suffrage down. This defeat for NASWA only threatened their state-by-state plan but spoke for the efficacy of the Anthony Amendment.

Though Alice would continue to flavor their wounds with salt, Catt's crew was not down yet.

### *Lagniappe: $ocialite $uffragists*

Alva Belmont had no trouble cashing in on both her husbands' fortunes. Before she divorced William

Kissam Vanderbilt, grandson of Cornelius Vanderbilt of boat and train fame, she built her summer "cottage" Marble House for $11 million (equivalent to $293 million in 2016). Fortunately, there was no divorce settlement for the Newport, Rhode Island 50 room mansion; it was Alva's outright, William's 39th birthday gift to her.

Then she married a rich financier, Oliver Hazard Perry Belmont, who'd she had met previously while cruising on Vanderbilt's yacht, the *Alva*. She shuttered the Marble House and moved down the street to his "cottage", Belacourt, whose entire first floor consisted of stables to house his favorite horses. (The Belmont name persists today in the Third Race of the Triple Crown at Belmont Racetrack in New York.)

Alva managed to make her mark in the exclusive social register that was New York's Gilded Age society. Though the Belmonts were wealthy enough, they were not included in the select 400 persons who could fit into the William and Caroline Astor's ballroom. The Astors did not associate with the newly rich. Canny Alva retaliated with a legendary costume ball whose guest list included the cream of New York society, but not the Astors. Suddenly, Caroline left her calling card at Alva's place.

Then in 1908, Oliver Belmont passed away and Alva reinvented herself once again. With her characteristic zeal and wit, she fully embraced the cause of Women's Suffrage. She acquainted herself with the Pankhursts and fancied their militant methods. Ultimately she found her way to Alice Paul and her Congressional Union. With Oliver gone, she reopened

Marble House and summer, 1914, hosted a grand CU conference in her newly built Chinese Tea House situated cliffside with a panoramic view of the Atlantic Ocean.

The CU evolved into The National Women's Party, and at its launch in 1916 Alva pledged to raise an incredible $500,000. When public opinion soured on the White House pickets, Alva sent Alice a $5000. check in support. Though Alva was always a Gilded Age Socialite, thanks to the Vanderbilt and Belmont fortunes, her sympathies and her checkbook were anchored in the suffragist cause

Unlike Alva Belmont's sympathy with the militant British suffragette, another New York socialite Katherine Duer Mackay embraced feminine wiles to peacefully promote women's right to vote. A leading member of the hidebound elite, she stressed and dressed to her 1913 femininity to counter arguments that declared the reason women wanted the vote was that they really wanted to be men. Ignoring convention, she formed the Equal Franchise Society an invitation-only organization "formed not to reach the masses but to invite the elite to experiment with a lady-like approach. It was dedicated to influencing the influential.... "[54]

Despite the New York Times Anti-Suffrage stance, those who might look to wealthy socialites for leadership would be inspired by their promotion of suffrage causes. Add the financial backing of colorful

---

[54] Neuman, Johanna, *Gilded Society* (New York, NY: Washington Mews Books, 2017) p.47

members of high society, and the role of the rich in shaping the success of women's right to vote is clear.

Alice Paul and Mrs. O.H.P. Bellmont 11/17/23 LC-DIG-npcc 24889

# Chapter 16
# A Car Ride from Hell

The new year,1915, started off on a sour note. President Wilson, ever anti, wrote to a friend. "Suffrage for women will absolutely no change in politics-it is the home that will be disastrously affected." [55] Somehow the brilliant professor saw allowing women to vote next step to home wrecking. He never explained how that might work.

Then the House of Representatives for the first time in history, on January 12th voted on a suffrage amendment. Maybe they were listening to the 200,000 members of the spanking new National Association Opposed to Women's Suffrage. Maybe the Prohibitionists had scared them off or maybe they agreed with their boss, because the vote tally resulted in a disappointing 204 nays, burying the suffragists' hopes. But Alice had another scheme, The Panama Pacific International Exposition had just opened its splendid display in San Francisco that January, 1915. The city had much to celebrate. Nine years before, in a devastating earthquake, the earth had rumbled and heaved and flattened everything there into a smoking heap. Now little of the devastation was evident. Life in the bustling town had begun again. With even more to mark, the exposition noted the completion of the Panama Canal in August, 1914, finished despite the

---

[55] Library of Congress, American Memory

formidable yellow fever, malaria, and engineering obstacles.

Progress was the life force of PPIE. For the first time in history the west coast would speak to the east coast over the amazing, new, transcontinental telephone. Visitors could stand by and watch the part by part creation of a Ford Motor Car. The company had installed an actual assembly line cranking out 25 new Model T's a day. Suffragist, young Hazel Hunkins dared not to refuse Alice and so found herself high above the fair, in a new-fangled flying machine, in a biplane dropping thousands of suffrage leaflets on the place below. The zeitgeist of the times demanded that the country build big and celebrate conspicuously. At 435 feet the exhibition's Tower of Jewels said it all; nothing was too bold or extravagant. In daylight the sun bounced off the 100,000 cut glass faceted "jewels"; at night 50 spotlights danced about the multi -colored gems, fire flies on steroids.

What then could be more progressive than women who voted? Alice took no time in cashing in on the fever, and sent Margaret Whittemore to the San Francisco site with a charge to open a CU exhibit, The Freedom Booth. She would stock it with banners and flags and all sorts of materials meant to boost the votes for women cause. For a year the Freedom Booth carried on a suffrage propaganda surge. It was a most accommodating spot, a place for women to lounge on the couches and be instructed in the suffragists' cause. They could also donate money while they rested, and often they did. Most persuasive  was the "petition," an yards-long paper roll which at fair's end had collected a half million supporters' signatures all aimed to persuade and overwhelm the President.

But how to deliver this most persuasive collection of suffragist sympathizers' names to Washington, DC?

Alice had no trouble laying big tasks on her followers. Her own unwavering self-confidence and resolve inspired her supporters and frightened her opponents. Her single-minded dedication to the cause of women was contagious, and often CU members found themselves in somewhat awkward situations, like Sara Bard Field and her erstwhile companion, Frances Joliffe did, charged with delivering the huge petition by carrying it across the continent's brand new Lincoln Highway. They would travel 3,000 miles in a new Overland Touring Car in the company of two strange lady strangers.

The first Women Voter's Convention, was orchestrated by the CU and not coincidentally held in San Francisco in the waning days of the Panama Pacific extravaganza. Its final day, September 4, hosted an incredibly star-studded cast of speakers, all suffragist supporters. Helen Keller spoke that day, accompanied by her mentor, Annie Sullivan Macey. Likewise presenting were such luminaries as former president, Theodore Roosevelt, famed evangelist Billy Sunday, actress Mabel Taliaferro, and educator, Maria Montessori. Clearly suffragists were supported across the spectrum.

## The Ride from Hell

Amid the bands and songs and cheers of those who weren't taking the trip, the Overland Touring Car departed San Francisco. Its primary mission was to demonstrate the political power of women voters in the twelve western states that in 1915 permitted enfranchisement for all. In addition, the travelling "envoys" task was to spread the suffragist message, with speeches on city street corners but also possibly delivered from the back seat of the car. They were to ingratiate themselves to town officials, and gather even more signatures. Mabel Vernon would precede the Overland by train. All arrangements would be in place, bands, auto parades, mayors and an occasional governor would be waiting.

Passenger Sara Bard Field, a 33-year-old wisp of a woman, might have viewed her fellow travelers with some concern. She feared Frances Joliffe would bail. She'd be alone with the drivers, two large Swedish women, Rhode Island residents, who made little effort to be pleasant and to speak English. They were willing to take Sara and Frances, and that was enough for Alice. Maybe not so much for Sara. She ventured, "But Alice I said, "do you realize that service stations across the country are very scarce, and you have to have a great deal of mechanical knowledge in case the car has something break down?"

"Oh well," she said 'if that happens, I'm sure some good man will come along to help you." In her enthusiasm for her cause, Alice was sometimes expedient and here even sexist, a false assumption in this case. The mechanical repairs would be handled by the lady riding shotgun, "mechanician", Ingabord Kindstedt.  For Alice, the opportunity to showcase CU political clout to the nation was irresistible.

And so as the din of their departing gala died, the massive Overland Touring Car set off for the barely completed Lincoln Highway.  They would sail forth on the very first girls only transcontinental automobile political expedition of all time.

Huddled in back, dressed warmly in a new fur collared travelling suit, Sara, a poet and writer, had mixed feelings. Though embarking on a lark, she might have been saddened at leaving her two children behind with their father, her divorced husband. Then for comfort, she might have run her fingers through the thick fur of her buffalo robe, a gift from her future mate, another poet. And she might also have wondered… what in the world am I doing here?

But the dauntless little crew headed north, and just before they left Sacramento and turned east for the Sierras and Reno, Frances bailed; she said she was sick. So it was only Sara and the big gals now.

The trip that followed was a tremendous success in terms of the suffragists' mission.  Mabel Vernon prepared their welcoming reception in the towns they would visit. Speeches were delivered, signatures were affixed to the petition. Votes for Women resounded through the streets of a string of cities and towns.

But the car ride itself would vary from miserable to a flat out matter of survival. By September 28, they were nine days and 380 miles into their journey. Well enough, so far, but they were about to drive into the 600-mile expanse of the Great American Desert, and their Lincoln Highway had evaporated. GPS was a hundred years in the future. There were some maps, but no one thought to pack one. And Mabel Vernon was expecting them in Salt Lake City. Somewhere, late in the day, outside a small town called Winnemucca they took a wrong turn. Years later Sara relived a night from hell.

Even wrapped up in her buffalo robe "the bitter cold of the night and the utter desolation of the whole country and the fear that we would not have enough gasoline to get to a filling station kept us agitated and in a good deal of physical distress."[60] Fortunately, the dim glow of sunrise finally revealed the low shape of a ranch house and safety.

As the trip proceeded Sara might have hoped that their combined struggle could on some level, endear her to the Swedes. But smoldering away, apparently jealous of Sara's many successful speeches and adoring receptions, the mechanician got mean, shooting foul looks and nasty gestures at the attractive suffragist. Sara tried to mollify the lady, but her Swedish was zero and their English was in the low teens. For the remainder of the trip, Sara shared space with a woman whose hatred was clear.

In Wyoming it was blizzards, with snow drifts so huge the ladies had to get out and push. Then it was the rain in Kansas when late one wet night the Overland suddenly dropped into an enormous water-filled hole. They were marooned and helpless crying out to the dark air for aid. Sara had spotted a farmhouse they'd passed and she took off into the night, slogging through the muddy road's ooze. The farmer, surprised at the soggy woman who appeared on his doorstep, graciously harnessed two staunch workhorses and pulled the auto and the waiting Swedes from out their wet depository.

Then things got worse.

Someplace around Cedar Rapids, Iowa, Sara must have had a particularly raucous reception and that unglued big Ingebord. She came close to Sara and leveling her eyes, slowly pronounced a death sentence for Sara. "At the end of this trip, I'm going to kill you."

Sara was flat out tired, tired of bouncing hard in the Overland, tired of street corner preaching and especially done with the threatening attitude of Miss Kindstedt. The driver, Miss Kindberg, tried desperately to comfort Sara, but the taunts and snarls continued. Sara had signed on as an envoy with message and as a newspaper reporter, not as a verbal dart board. Around Des Moines, she wrote a letter of resignation to Alice. Alice offered money, "Pay Field whatever necessary enable her to continue trip to end." Sara turned down the money.

Why Sara kept on is a tribute to her courage and zeal for the suffragists' cause and of Alice's persuasive powers. It was all Alice's fault she wrote "You must not inspire people with such confidence in their powers as you did me." Or maybe because she was simply unaware of the fact that Ingabord had only recently been released from a mental institution

Frances finally rejoined Sara in Albany, well enough for the homestretch. The Misses K. had bailed in Rhode Island. They'd take a rest and ship the

Overland to New York. Though a recent suffrage referendum had been defeated in New York, Sara and Frances were received in the city with a grand Fifth Avenue parade, a flower bedecked motorcade flying golden balloons.

## Triumphal Entry?

Then the final stretch, onto DC with more parades and speeches in Newark, and Philadelphia and finally Baltimore. In Hyattsville, on the edge of Washington they stepped off to lead the grand procession which would crown the Overland's passengers 3,000-mile journey. Rested now, the Swedish duo joined Sara and Frances along with Mabel Vernon in the sturdy old Overland, proudly displaying the tattered suffragist's banner. Each suffrage state was represented by the commanding presence of a proud woman astride a tall horse. Women wearing purple, white and gold marched precisely in a perfect replica of the Liberty Bell. Finally, the resounding statement of support, the petition bearing the multitude of signatures appeared at parade's end. Carried widespread, twenty marchers, ceremoniously climbed the alabaster Capitol's steps and presented its message to the congressmen, the suffrage sympathizers, who stood in waiting.

Alice Paul, the orchestrator of this miracle journey, remained quietly apart. Its success was her pleasure, not accolades. Praise was premature for Alice. She had a president to convert.

Wilson did receive the petition and gave it lip service, He promised yes he'd vote for the Anthony Amendment in Congress, but just not *this* Congress. His attention was rightfully drawn elsewhere as war raged in Europe, and so he wondered, did America have a dog in that fight? Well maybe.  Just last May a German U-boat had sunk the English liner, Lusitania, and 128 Americans had died. With such an immediate problem did he really have time for women's suffrage?  Alice felt that he did.

Also, he was up for reelection in the next year, 1916.

## *Lagniappe:  A Very Brief History of Cars or Ten Facts You Might Not Know about Cars*

1.-The very first cars in the 1700's were powered by steam engines.

2.-The very first gas driven car, the Benz Patent *Motorwagon*, was invented over 120 years ago, in 1885, by German engineer, Karl Benz. It had three wire wheels and was difficult to control. It crashed into a wall during its demonstration. On the third version of the *Motorwagon*, Benz improved the design by switching to wooden wheels.

3.-The 1926 Benz auto, the *Mercedes Benz* was named after Mercedes, the ten-year-old daughter of Benz' business associate, Emil Jellinck.

4.-American Ransom E. Olds', *Oldsmobile.* sported a one cylinder, three horsepower engine, steered by a tiller, and was available to the average American for $650. In 1910, the *Limited Touring,* a luxury model, ($4,600.) included such options as a speedometer, a clock and a full glass windshield.

5.-Many car makers jumped into the sales market and by 1908 there were 253. The number dropped to 44 in 1929, with 80% of the market owned by Ford, Chrysler and General Motors.

6.-A shortage of skilled labor contributed to Henry Ford's use of a moving assembly line and, in 1913, the mass produced *Model T.* When it was withdrawn in 1927, it was available for $290.

7.-To compete with the Model T, makers of moderately priced cars allowed buyers to purchase "on time," initiating the installment plan option still used today.

8.-With sales stalling due to market saturation, Alfred P. Sloan Jr. introduced the infamous, "Planned Obsolescence." He believed that the main objective of the manufacturer was to make money not just to make motorcars. Each year a slightly different version of his cars was trotted out. Owners would be embarrassed by the increasing "age" of their autos.

9.- While the 1960s big three automakers emphasized profit over quality, the American car buyer got bitten by the German Volkswagen "bug" and the compact, efficient, Japanese imports.

10.- Modern Day Cars parallel park themselves, driverless cars let you nap in a traffic jam, electric cars plug in like a toaster.
What's next? Cars that fly?

# Chapter 17

# Democratic Stranglehold

**Deputation**: *A person or group appointed to represent other or others.*

In the early 1900's it was perfectly possible for ordinary citizens to speak directly to the President of the United States. The suffragists did and were generally politely received by the President, and then dismissed. Wilson's responses to the repeated appeals arced from bored, to tolerant, to finally, animosity

Alice was ready to bite the hand that fed her, the Democratic Party.  She was an equal opportunity offender and saw the party in power as the party responsible. Her strategy was to use publicity to ridicule and damage the Democratic party and President Woodrow Wilson. She'd use adverse public opinion to shame them into supporting the Anthony Amendment.

She'd formulated her plan at Alva Belmont's Marble House back in August, 1914.  CU would send two organizers to every suffrage state to mobilize women voters to oppose any Democrat candidate because the Democratic Party traditionally had blocked passage of the suffrage amendment. If enough women in suffrage states voted against the Democratic Party in the coming elections, as a result then the congressional Democrats would change their attitude on suffrage. "When we have once affected the result in a national election, no party will trifle with suffrage any longer."

Crafty Alice wanted to frame the issue of women's suffrage as a prominent campaign issue. With national attention congressmen could no longer trivialize women's rights. The defeat of the Suffrage Amendment in January only strengthened Alice's resolve. She'd quit leadership of the CU and hit the road. She was good at raising money and the CU was in desperate need of funds. But no one would take her place. So she left anyway. Lucy would be in charge. She would tour the country along with other loyal CU members. They would attempt to confront the 531 members of Congress on their home turf. Their reception was not always wonderful. Democrats hadn't forgiven their attempts to oppose them.

The CU was emerging as a political power and Catt wanted part of the action, on her terms. With the enthusiasm generated by their first national convention in December, Alice and Lucy thought maybe, just maybe the National and CU could work together rather than at cross purposes. They agreed to meet with its eternally disapproving NASWA. Then Catt told Alice she'd have to give up her election policy; she must stop holding the Democrats responsible. When Alice refused Catt rose immediately and stalked out of the room, leaving Alice and Lucy staring at an empty chair "I will fight you to the last ditch," she hissed as the door shut behind her.

Shortly after, Anna Howard Shaw, a most admirable woman, who was more virtuous than organized, finally resigned from her presidency of the NASWA Carrie Chapman Catt, longtime circling Shaw, swooped in to replace her. Several recent state suffrage referendums had been defeated causing the practical Catt to change her adamant stand for a state-by-state approach. Suddenly she saw the light and Alice Paul was in it.

Then on April 1, 1915 headlines on the New York Times screamed, "Women Organize New Suffrage Move." The article went on to state "it means a new national organization which will take from the old national movement much of its young blood and enthusiastic young, radical workers…There should be an initiation fee of 25 cents."

Men would be barred from membership in the planned new party though the Times recorded a lively exchange. "We've been working for sixty years without men, why should we include them now?" asked Mrs. Belmont.

"Shouldn't we allow them to use their direct or indirect influence?" asked a woman in the audience amidst much laughter.

"Let them use their direct or indirect influence if they'd like," returned Mrs. Belmont. "but don't admit them to the Union."

131

"Ladies, we find ourselves in the unique position of disfranchising men," said Mrs. Donald Hooker of Baltimore.[56]

## Meanwhile

"Location, location, location," was Alva Belmont's mantra, so in November, she bought a well-situated mansion for Alice and the CU. "You could hear the exquisite China dishes rattle each day on the close White House table," wrote one journalist. Alice said thank you to Alva, The Cameron House did have much to offer in addition to its stone's throw distance from the White House. Its eleven bedrooms could be rented, likewise its meeting rooms. Then there was the snob appeal. Wealthy patrons would be impressed with the CU's apparent prosperity and Cameron House could appear as a symbol of propriety. There was ample space for suffragists to mingle. Friendships were formed: principles were affirmed and nascent suffragists would be baptized in the incredible resolve that would forge the future "Iron Jawed Angels."

President Wilson had his own set of problems. In addition to the tragic sinking of the Lusitania in May, a possible war harbinger, and death of his wife in August 1914, left him single and searching for love. Though Wilson actually craved the company of women, he would stay securely superior to those women who rarely confronted him. His first teaching position at Bryn Mawr, a woman's college, had him disparaging his students as unfit for stringent learning, though

---

[56] New York Times "Women Organize New Suffrage Move." *New York Times* 1 April 1915:24

"demure, friendly damsels." With his vision of women as being mostly dim but useful, Alice Paul's personality and methods must have been particularly irksome. He had a country to run. For him women should just stay simple, much less vote.

Though generally of a demeaning mindset about women, he had been desperate for a wife. Edit Galt, who claimed direct descent from Pocahontas, and a wealthy widow of a jewelry magnate had become his obsession. He would write to her several times a day, pleading with her to marry him. She wanted to wait until after the election. It would appear unseemly to marry so soon after Ellen's death. The Wilsons were wed in December, 1915.

Edith was intelligent and well spoken. Although definitely not a suffragist, she was politically involved. The Presidents' advisors did not see the office of the presidency as a family business. Woodrow did, and Edith sat in the Oval Office while governmental business was conducted. It was as well she did, because when Woodrow became incapacitated with a stroke, in October, 1919, she is reputed to having run the country in his stead; Edith insisted that the President was only suffering from temporary exhaustion and that all important business should be sent to her. Some said she signed his signature without his knowledge. Edith denied it all. She blamed the President's political opponents.

A woman, Edith Wilson, running the nation as virtual president was the ultimate irony in the country which would not allow her to vote.

# Chapter 18

## A Political Party Rises and a Star Dies

The hostile response of Democrats to Alice's war against the "party in power" could hardly come as a shock. In yet another attempt to move the suffrage bill out of the House Judiciary Committee, Alice presented her case to a phalanx of angry representatives.

Joseph Taggart of Kansas attacked. "You didn't defeat a single Democratic member of Congress in a suffrage state." (Taggart was not reelected)

With consummate poise, Alice drew in a breath, leveled her eyes at the congressman and answered in slow measured tones. "Why, then, are you so stirred up over our campaign?"

Furious, Taggart continued to question. "You are organized, are you not, for the chastisement of political parties who do not do your bidding at once.?"

Alice spelled out her strategy in a simple statement. "We are organized to win votes from women who have the vote, to help other women to get it."

This exchange took place in December, 1915. The House Judiciary Committee thereupon decided to do nothing until after the election in 1916. Alice would have to find ways to keep the pressure on Congress and in the American public's eye.

Ever resourceful, she envisioned a train car loaded with suffragists, crossing America, singing the praises of women's votes, and with a full head of steam and a noisy departure, Alice's plan took off. On April 9, Washington's Union Station resounded with the clamor of bands and banners and stirring songs. Women arrived in cars festooned with flowers and bedecked in purple, white and yellow ribbons. With all the pomp of a presidential parade, 24 determined women marched through the cold air and boarded The *Suffragist Special*. Theirs was a mission of persuasion which had a lot to do with addressing crowds from the train's rear platform, mixing with the local politicians, raising money and more. Lucy Burns ascended to the heavens, aloft in a hydroplane, then she dropped pamphlets from 1,000 feet onto the place below.

Lucy Burns at Seattle,(1916) LC DIG ggbain 22581

But not every city loved the suffragists; their reception in Chicago was nasty. In contrast though, back east the Suffrage Movement was burgeoning and Alice knew her time had come. Her organization could no longer be just the CU, noisy as it was. She needed a bite of the big enchilada. She needed a political party to counter the influence of the established parties. Alice was going big time now. The Suffrage Amendment was wrapped in mothballs somewhere in the congressional attic, and an election was imminent. Congressional feet needed to be put to the fire. What was begun back in April 1915 she would complete on June 5, 1916.

The call went out. Thousands of women heard it and gathered in Chicago for a grand convention. Copy Catt was listening too. A *Suffrage Special* copycatt, she sent out an anemic one car, cross-country tour ambitiously named the *"Golden Flier."* Then she surprised Alice with a NASWA convention and parade, oddly and deliberately scheduled at the same time as Alice's convention. "We're not trying to steal anyone's thunder," Catt announced to a reporter, she'd planned her convention months ago she claimed; she just hadn't mentioned it to the press, and she couldn't resist a dig, "I consider our methods infinitely better than theirs." To shortsighted Mrs. Catt, Alice and Lucy remained the enemy. They should just go away.

## Women's Very Own Political Party

Unperturbed Alice launched her convention and the National Women's Party was officially born and lives to today, headquartered in Washington, DC.[57] "For the first time in history, women came together to organize their political power into a party to free their own sex. For the first time in history representatives of men's political parties came to plead before these women voters for the support of their respective parties."[58] Alva Belmont liked the use of "National." She stated "The word 'National' added to anything seems to impress the general mind with more importance." It was a shrewd observation of a practice which persists.

---

[57] Nationalwomansparty.org
[58] Stevens, Doris, *Jailed for Freedom,* 18

---

This was the game plan. The NWP's only objective would be the immediate passage of the Anthony Amendment and furthermore, only women who already had the vote could join. November elections were nearing and Alice opined that the clout of the four million women who could vote would influence the election of the president. But, unfortunately for Alice, she was from NJ, and voteless and though she couldn't join the political party she founded, those women from the twelve suffrage states could. Doris Stevens reported from the scene, and she determined that the NWP would "punish politically any party in power which did not use its power to free women. They, the NWP would be "a party which would become a potent power of protest in the following election."

It worked. Finally, both the Republican and Democratic parties had gotten scared enough to pay serious attention to women's rights. Though their gestures were vague, as in the Republican Party Plank, or state centered, like the Democratic Party Plank, the big guys begrudgingly had to acknowledge the collective clout of determined women.

Wilson continued to speak out with earnest conviction from both sides of his presidential mouth. Though professing support for the suffrage amendment, in fact he had authored the Democratic Party's state by state plank. A southern soul, from a southern state, he had confided to Harriot Blatch just previously, about "The negro question."[59] Passage impossible, had to be

---

[59] President Wilson's Record, *Suffragist*, 23 September 5; Editorials In Suffragist, 16 September, 1916, 5,8, Dubois, HSB 197

his aim. "Patience" was his mantra. Ladies should just wait until he had sorted out the issue of the war in Europe and its ramifications for the U.S.. Ladies reminded him that same post-Civil War promise had left the abolitionist/suffragists voteless too.

## A Great Trick and A Great Tragedy

Through an almost miraculous series of events, Alice was able to snare five seats in Congress while President Wilson was delivering his speech extolling the suffrage just granted in the Philippines, to men. As he went on Mabel Vernon seated in the balcony, unbuttoned the large coat she wore, reached in and opened a giant belt pin. She nodded to the ladies alongside her and as one, they stood, unpinned and unfurled a banner. The assembly gasped as the large yellow banner dropping from the balcony beseeching Wilson with their eternal question, "Mr. President, what will you do for women's suffrage?"

For just a minute the words beamed at the astonished speaker until the door keeper recovered his shock and grabbed the banner from the jubilant ladies. So, with mission accomplished, the ladies were escorted from the chamber. But the dramatic moment was captured by the press. Alice was delighted at the buzz created by the incident. Her aim, as ever, was to keep women's rights in the public eye.

Then sadly, fate altered the scene. Shortly after the convention Alice had sent The Suffrage Special train across the west to force the Democratic candidates' into taking a stance on suffrage. A stream of powerful speakers would follow them, including Harriot Stanton Blatch, Sara Bard of Cross Country ride

fame, and, most compelling, the charismatic Inez
Milholland (Boissevain). She, the famous horsewoman
who led the 1913 march, would draw crowds as a
special "Flying Envoy." She would swoop across the 12
suffrage states and with her star quality draw attention
to the cause. Alice scheduled Inez for a whopping 32
cities is 30 days unaware of the fact that the young
beauty's health was failing.

Inez Milholland knew when she began the trip
that she didn't feel so good. She knew that Alice was
asking too much of her; she went anyway. She was the
same lady who when her alma mater, Vassar, rejected
her as a speaker, held a great rally by scaling the walls
of an adjacent graveyard. But try as she would Inez
just couldn't deliver. Increasingly she cancelled
appearances, claiming tonsillitis. Alice, reluctant to lose
her star performer but respecting her apparent neediness
shortened Inez' schedule and suggested she just be a
presence on the stage while another suffragist delivered
the message. Inez wasn't too sick to let that happen, at
least that's what she thought. Then she collapsed mid
speech in Los Angeles, but to cheers, later was carried
back to deliver her words while seated.

Inez died, on November 25. She was 31 years
old. It might have been pernicious anemia or maybe a
heart attack or a stroke. It didn't matter what, the young
beauty was dead. A woman who had in fact, given her
life for the cause of women. Her iconic portrait of the
bold horsewoman leading the parade of determined
marchers foretold the impending clash. Her last
conscious words said it all and became the suffragists'
battle cry... *How long must women wait for liberty?*

With Inez' death Alice knew she had a martyr and felt a patriot deserved a hero's acclaim. Fortunately, business must have been slack at Christmas time in the Capitol because Alice was able to reserve the National Statuary Hall of the Capitol's Rotunda for a grand Inez Milholland Memorial Service. Inez, large in life, would be even larger in death

So as the sweet voices of a boys' choir wafted through the chamber's vaulted ceiling that December 25$^{th}$, a young girl dressed in white entered, bearing aloft the very same banner Inez had flaunted in the New York Suffrage March. Guests breathing in the heady aroma of pine boughs and laurel, marveled at the ensuing procession of girls bearing the purple, white and gold colors of the suffrage cause, and waving the banners of the Congressional Union. Standing tall, Maud Younger spoke for the Women's Party, eulogizing the bold, young woman who was the suffragists' icon. Inez' early death was proclaimed the outcome of her zeal for women's rights, and the life and times of the "most beautiful" suffragist was duly celebrated by a thousand mourners. For one day, at least, a woman's mission was elevated to equality with the host of dead males memorialized all about in marble.

## The "Most Beautiful Suffragist

Inez Milholland (1886-1916) disregarded all of the prevailing female mores, and she did so with style, starting in college, Vassar. Because suffrage meetings were forbidden, she held "classes" to inform her fellow students regarding women's rights, at one time off campus, in a graveyard. By graduation she had received so much notoriety that the New York Times sent a columnist to report on her exploits.

No matter her brilliance, Harvard, Yale, Cambridge and Oxford all rejected her application to Law School. But the "males only" attitude did not pertain at New York University, and she received her law degree in 1912. Thereafter she submerged herself into activism, advocating for a wide variety of causes, from prison reform to labor issues. Equality for all was her mantra and found her a member of the NAACP and Alice Paul's National Women's Party.

Liberated, her personal life allowed her the freedom to engage in uninhibited love affairs. She deliberately courted fellow radical, lawyer Max Eastman, confessed her love and asked him to elope with her. Though their torrid love affair ended when he finally agreed, Inez moved on falling in and out of love until she proposed marriage after a month acquaintance, to Eugen Jan Boissevain. His acceptance did not insure fidelity but it did preclude Inez from any right to vote. Since she had married a Dutchman, her citizenship was revoked.

Inez Milholland went on to become the flamboyant icon of women's demonstrations. Newspapers celebrated the beautiful young woman who always led suffrage parades. On March 3,1913, a crown on her lustrous hair, and a white cape flying, she opened the turbulent women's parade. Astride the massive stallion "Grey Dawn", she cleared the crowds for the embattled women, fending off protestors, and cementing her exotic reputation as the epitome of the liberated New Woman.

Though for years her zeal for the suffrage cause had her to disregard her health, and despite her pernicious anemia she determined to undertake the fatal Western speaking tour in 1916. Mid speech, in October on stage in Los Angeles, Inez collapsed and sadly, despite every effort to save her with repeated blood transfusions, she died on November 25, 1916, a wild and wonderful life extinguished.

With appropriate glamour she was honored by a thousand mourners in an Inez Milholland Memorial Service in the United States Capitol Rotunda, on December 25. 1916. Though a bright light had died, a martyr for suffrage was born.

# Chapter 19

## Enough Woodrow, Suffragists Get Mad

It was the right time to strike. Public sympathy was with the suffragists, and Alice opined that President Wilson was ripe for the picking. So on January 9, 1917 she sent over a deputation of 300 women ostensibly to present "Milholland Memorials" to the President. Wilson had agreed to only one speaker and as the 299 remaining women stood quietly, little Sara Bard, the cross country survivor, would speak truth to power on tip toes. Doris Stevens was there and she recorded their exchange.

Bard: We have come here to you in the name of justice, in the name of democracy, in the name of all women who have fought and died for this cause. We have come asking you this day to speak some favorable word to us that we may know that you will use your good and great office to end this wasteful struggle of women.

Wilson: Ladies, I had not been apprised that you were coming here to make any representations that would issue an appeal to me...I, therefore, am not prepared to say anything further than I have said on previous occasions of this sort. It is impossible for me, until the orders of my party are changed, to do anything other than I am doing as a party leader. I have done my best and continue to do my best in the interest of a cause in which I personally believe. [60]

Eyes widened in disbelief. Everyone present, including himself, knew that Woodrow always got from his party what Woodrow wanted. For some reason, today he talked big but refused to help. Harriot Blanch might have reflected back on a private meeting in July, 1916, when Wilson told her sotto voce that if women got the vote, in two states, " the blacks would still preponderate."[61]

Stevens continues, The President stood for a brief instant as if waiting for some faint stir of approval which did not come…Then he turned abruptly on his heel and left 300 suffragists staring at a closed door.

## Enough, Woodrow

Flabbergasted the women trekked back across Lafayette Square and reconvened in headquarters, the Cameron House.  Harriot Blatch had it up to here and she spoke. …Never before did the Democratic Party lie more in the hands of one man than it lies today in the hands of President Wilson. He controls his party, and I don't think he is too modest to know it.

…We can't organize bigger and more influential deputations. We can't organize bigger processions. We

---

[60] Stevens, Doris. *Jailed for Freedom*, 25.
[61] Blatch and Lutz, *Challenging Years,269.*

can't, women, do anything more in that line. We have got to take new departure. …We have got to begin and begin immediately.

Women it rests with us…Won't you come and join us in standing day after day at the gates of the White House with banners asking, "What will you do, Mr. President, for one-half the people of this nation?

Stand there as sentinels-sentinels of liberty, sentinels of self-government, silent sentinels. Let us stand beside the gateway where he must pass in and out, so that he can never fail to realize that there is a tremendous earnestness and insistence back of this measure.[62]

Alice just listened and had to smile. Wilson's intransigence was always good for publicity.

## Silent Sentinels Are Born, Quietly

Then as if by magic, on the very next day, January 10, twelve women appeared at the gates of the White House. Having processed single file, arm's length apart, with their gold, white and purple sashes and banners dazzling in the midmorning sun, they had assembled at the White House gates.   The women positioned themselves, on each side of the East and West White House Gates, a colorful astonishment to Washington's world. The weather was warm, they were not illegal, and the guards were just amused. Even when Wilson's limousine passed by, returning him from his daily golf game, there was no incident.   The national press took

---

[62] Ibid

note, (check off publicity, Alice) and life was good for Silent Sentinels on that mild winter's day.

But if Alice was seated in one of the cozy leather wingchairs in the males only Cosmos Club overlooking the suffragists' site, she could have used the members' likely reaction as a crystal ball's forecast of things to come. The Sentinels giggled to see the men as they peered through the windows down their long, privileged noses, surrounded by the stuffed heads and horns of their past hunting prey. The picketers imagined them grousing at the "unsexed" women bearing inflammatory banners rather than aprons.

The Silent Sentinels, arrived from all parts of the country, planning to harry the President each day until his second term's inauguration in March. Day after day, from January 10th on, they appeared at the White House gates, but their daily protest began to be resented and papers, especially the *Washington Post* and the *New York Times* became vociferous in their condemnation.

Picketer Doris Stevens, took a more sanguine view. "The press cartoonists, by their friendly and satirical comments, helped a great deal in popularizing the campaign. In spite of the bitter editorial comment of most of the press, the humor of the situation had an almost universal appeal." [63] Alice on the defensive might say that no publicity is "bad" publicity. The worst fate is being ignored. Laugh at it or assail it, the whole country would know the cause of suffrage for women, and that was the point.

---

[63] Stevens, Doris. *Jailed for Freedom, ed O'Hare, Carol* (Troutdale, Oregon, New Sage Press, 1995). p. 63

---

But as Washington's temperature slid downward, Alice's fortunes continued to decline. Not surprisingly, the women's initial enthusiasm was being tried. Icy days had descended on Washington, and ankle length coats didn't help their feet, though often a concerned woman brought them hot bricks to stand on, and mittens, fur pieces, hot coffee, and raincoats sometimes too. With foul winter weather, with snow and sleet beating down mercilessly, women shifting foot to foot on boards, sharing the one donated fur coat, the indomitable Silent Sentinels kept faith. Six days a week they bore the price of their belief. Alice took pity and cut their hours from four to two.

As the Sentinels kept faith, Alice's base began to erode. Many Congressional Union members disagreed with the more militant tactics and attacked Alice with vehemence. Letters poured into the Cameron House, condemning the movement as useless, or unseemly for ladies, or at best counterproductive. Stalwart Lucy Burns had left for New York. CU members quit in protest. Even Harriot Blatch, whose big idea it was anyway, dropped out, angry at the inclusion of voting women in the troop.

No one was surprised at Carrie Chapman Catt's comment. Ever fawning over Wilson, she expressed concern regarding the "annoyance" and "embarrassment" for the president. She, like the president, paid lip service to passage of the Anthony Amendment, but still advocated for the useless state by state method. Yet, the unkindest cut came from Alice's own mother. Tacie Paul's wish delivered by post, "I hope thee will call it off."

---

But, as ever, Alice persisted. Though her prospects dimmed, Alice's incredible resolve never wavered, and occasionally the clouds parted to let in some sun. Alva Belmont's fat check arrived, staving off empty coffers, and more CU members abided than departed. With the sentinels' daily appearance at the White House becoming unremarkable, Alice resurrected public attention again by the invention of picketing days for special interest groups. The first State Day was Maryland Day, followed by College Day. Teacher's Day boasted of attendance by almost every state in the union. Patriotic Day brought loyal American institutions and Professional Day was attended by a growing number of women doctors and lawyers and nurses.

Then, more good news, Alice's long term admirer, William Parker, came to town and settled in DC. His support and company was warmly welcomed by the embattled Alice and they spent several evenings together. It's easy to imagine the comfort to Alice of William's devoted presence, and he stayed on in Washington.

Good friends are always in good taste, but Alice had miles to go before she'd sleep.

149

## Chapter 20
## Wilson's Two Nightmares…War and Women

After Germany had sunk the British liner, RMS Lusitania with 128 American passengers aboard, in May, 1915, Wilson got mad and made them promise never to do that again. They kept their promise, but didn't say they wouldn't sink U.S. merchant ships, and they did. Beginning in January, 1917, seven ships were scuttled by German submarines.

Then there was the Zimmerman Telegram which was intercepted by the British and sent to America in January, 1917. The telegram noted that some deranged German strategist had concocted a plan whereby Mexico would enter the war on Germany's side and in exchange, Germany would give them back Texas, New Mexico and Arizona. Somehow Mexico managed to resist the offer, but President Wilson was incensed. In February he severed relations with Germany: war was now unavoidable. It had only to be declared by Congress.

Woodrow Wilson, would be inaugurated into his second term as the United States President and Alice and her crew intended to be there for the action. They planned to present the president with the resolutions passed at the National Women's Party's just completed convention. Doris Stevens recorded the day in chagrin.

In our optimism we hoped that this glorified picket pageant might form a climax to our three months of picketing.

Inauguration Day, March 4, 1917 was a day of high wind and stinging, icy rain. A thousand women marched, …in rain soaked garments, hands bare, gloves torn by the sticky varnish from the banner poles and streams of water running down the poles into the palms of their hands. …. Two bands managed to continue their spirited music in spite of the driving rain.

…Most extraordinary precautions had been taken about the White House. There were almost as many police officers as marchers. …For more than two hours the women marched, circling the White House four times… the cold almost unendurable…hoping to the last moment that their leaders would be allowed to take in to the President the resolutions they were carrying.

It was only when they saw the presidential limousine, in the late afternoon, roll luxuriously out of the grounds and through the gates down Pennsylvania Avenue, that the weary marchers realized that President Wilson had deliberately turned them away unheard…President and Mrs. Wilson looked straight ahead as if the long line of purple, white and gold was invisible.

All the women who took part in that march will tell you of the passionate resentment that burned in their hearts on that dreary day. This one incident more than any other probably did more than any other to make

151

women sacrifice themselves…. Three months of picketing had not been enough. We must continue on duty at his gates but also at the gates of Congress. [64]

As winter waned, war clouds gathered and hung over an anxious nation. With the looming crisis, suffragists were presented with a quandary. Did suffrage for women pale in importance to the national threat? Should the CU's energy be redirected toward the war effort? Members were conflicted.

Alice wasn't. Quakers are pacifists. (See the classic movie, *High Noon*) Alice was still nominally a Quaker, ergo, for Alice, she would logically advocate for… suffrage. Wait a minute, people said wondering how Alice could set that conclusion straight.

Hers wasn't a simple response, but came as the result of single minded pursuit of her ideal and more so, her knowledge of American history. To those who would say if they could only postpone suffrage, they would be rewarded for their war efforts with the vote when peace came, she would point to the women who set aside their efforts until after the Civil War. They, Stanton and Anthony and all were rewarded with the U.S. Constitution's 15th Amendment, which gave black men the right to vote. All women, black or white, were excluded. Thank you, Congress, Alice might have thought. Fool me once, shame on you. Fool me twice, shame on me.

Carrie Chapman Catt always deferring to Wilson, declared NASWA's support in the event of war. She was different. Forgetting the intransigency of

---

[64] Stevens, ed. O'Hare p.66

southerners, she believed the president and suggested he might like to wait longer for a solution to suffrage. He replied that "This is not the opportune time." Not willing to wait, rejecting Catt's caving, her NASWA members left in droves to join the CU which had taken no official stance.

So Alice must thread that elusive needle. She must find the way to satisfy CU's western advocates of engagement in war, while staying aloof of the war effort.

Alice's CU umbrella covered all types. To those suffragists conflicted, she instructed that each person was free to work for peace or join in war preparations; the Union would neither sanction nor endorse either action. Basically, for Alice votes for women was still the largest issue at stake but, with a foot in both worlds, she felt she must find a way to relate suffrage to the war effort. Canny Alice found it. If women are to affect the war's decision they must have the vote.

Reflecting her innate Quaker pacifism, Alice switched her suffrage hat for a Quaker bonnet and visited Jeanette Rankin, the first woman to be elected to Congress and a confirmed pacifist. Alice enjoined Rankin, a Representative from Montana, to vote against war, declaring "it would be a tragedy for the first woman ever in Congress to vote for war; the only thing that seemed to us clear was that the women were the peace-loving half of the world and that by giving power to women we would diminish the possibilities of war.' [65]

---

[65] Fry, Conversations with Alice Paul, p.150

---

But with Germany's continued harassment, war seemed inevitable. On April 2, 1917 President Wilson addressed a joint session of Congress and issued his scripted mandate, words intended for history, "the world must be made safe for democracy." He concluded his address with a call to fight "for the rights of those who submit to authority, to have a voice in their own Government…"

*Really Woodrow? See any conflict here?*

Then after deliberating for four days, on April 6, Congress agreed with the President, and declared war. Jeanette Rankin, despite intense pressure from Catt, voted no and left the chamber in tears.

But was Wilson so oblivious to the notion of suffrage that he didn't recognize the contradiction in his own speech? He made it so easy for Alice to point out the fact that while he advocated passionately for worldwide democracy, he rejected it at home. Preventing women, citizens, the right to participate in their own government, was clearly a violation of democracy. This obvious oxymoron would shortly be the lever which would pry open Pandora's Box.

Slowly though, even with his notion of a proper woman's subservient place, he finally realized the war effort depended a great deal on women. The US Navy was first to recruit. About 12,000 women, took over male positions, many clerical, thus freeing men for combat, and though his southern bias resented black women's votes, he didn't refuse their service either, including them as Yeoman (F)s. Finally, Wilson chose an all-male delegation, headed by J.A.H. Hopkins, a millionaire from New Jersey, to declare that now the war had changed the suffrage question.

Words, words, words…the Silent Sentinels wanted more. The President should support the Senate's Suffrage Committee's move to consider suffrage support as a war measure. He claimed, however, that though the suffrage question was always on his mind, the program for the session was practically complete and it didn't include votes for women. What with so many war measures to consider, there was little time to process less important matters.

Into their sixth month now, the sentinels continued to stand outside the White House. The manifestations of popular approval of suffrage, the constant stream of protests to the administration against its delay nationally, and the shame of having women begging at its gates, could result in only one of two things. It must either pass the amendment or remove those troublesome pickets.

No problem here. He'd "Make the world safe for democracy." He'd remove the pickets.

Done.

# Part Five: The Descent into Hell (1917)

## Chapter 21

### Jailed for "Loud or Boisterous Talking"

No one dared to call it blatant hypocrisy, but the Sentinels were furious. They were actually reacting to a speech delivered in Russia by Envoy Elihu Root in which he commented that American leaders were elected by "universal, equal, direct, and secret suffrage."[66] Cameron house roiled with anger. What part of his "universal and direct" included women? This latest insult was simply a bridge too far and it brought out the banner response in newly returned Lucy Burns.

It was a big banner. So large Lucy and Doris Lewis were driven to the White House gates. Midday on June 20th they set themselves up alongside the entrance just before the Russian delegation arrived. The ten-foot spectacle said it all, and boldly broadcast its message, including the following:

WE, THE WOMEN OF AMERICA TELL YOU THAT AMERICA IS NOT A DEMOCRACY. TWENTY MILLION AMERICAN WOMEN ARE DENIED THE RIGHT TO VOTE, PRESIDENT

---

[66] NYT, 17 June 1917

WILSON IS THE CHIEF OPPONENT OF THEIR NATIONAL ENFRANCHISEMENT.

In wartime it was easy to confuse dissention with disloyalty. That day, righteous men and some naughty boys attacked, and immediately after the Russians passed, tore the banner from its bearers' hand, defaming them with lewd insults and gestures. Though the press was quick to condemn the banner, the damage to Wilson had been done. Alice had crossed a line. The women had exposed his vulnerability; his position was indefensible in the face of their continued presence. The cause of suffrage was once again, big news.

To those who accused the picketers of disrespect for America in the presence of a foreign government, Alice answered. "The intolerable conditions against which we protest can be changed in a twinkling of an eye. The responsibility for our protest is therefore with the Administration and not with the women of America. If the lack of democracy at home weakens the Administration in its fight for democracy three thousand miles away."[67] It was a standard enactment of the old saw demanding that the world should "do as I say, not do as I do."

On the following day, the Sentinel's continued their vigil with yet another Russian Banner. Immediately it was ripped from their hands. Clearly, they embarrassed the administration and their irksome presence needed to be ended, but how? The 1914 Clayton Antitrust Act had made picketing legal. The Silent Sentinels knew they

---

[67] Stevens, ed. O' Hare, p.74

157

had every right to be exactly where they were, and they weren't leaving anytime soon.

Shortly, the administration's forbearance under the public condemnations wore out. Though it was rumored that President Wilson feared adverse publicity resulting from the government's interference with the suffragist's legitimate free expression of speech, it was determined that the unrelenting criticism must be ended. The women had to be accused of something illegal, there must be some law out there that they had violated.

Finding that misdeed fell to the youngest ever police chief, Raymond Pullman, successor to the infamous Richard Sylvester, and ironically a former spokesman for suffrage. On the evening of June 21 he appeared at the door of the Cameron House. Sternly, he warned Alice. She must stop those infernal pickets or he will arrest them. Alice refused because she knew she was getting to President Wilson, and also, she welcomed the publicity which followed police intervention, a lesson well learned at the hands of the British suffragette.

We have picketed for six months without interference," said Miss Paul. Has the law been changed?

"No," was the reply, "but you must stop."

"But Major Pullman, we have consulted our lawyers and know we have a legal right to picket."

"I warn you, you will be arrested if you attempt to picket again."

_____

Who could argue against that kind of logic, so next morning, like Whack-a-mole, two women appeared at the White House, bravely brandishing yet another banner. It set out Woodrow Wilson's own lofty statements advocating for the international cause of democracy in blatant contrast to his failure to support that same cause at home.

WE WILL FIGHT FOR THE THINGS WE HAVE ALWAYS HELD NEAREST OUR HEARTS, FOR DEMOCRACY, FOR THE RIGHT OF THOSE WHO SUBMIT TO AUTHORITY TO HAVE A VOICE IN THEIR OWN GOVERNMENTS.

That bright spring morning, Lucy Burns and Katherine Morey knew they were in for trouble. They were a colossal affront to the president's pronouncements of rectitude, even though they quoted him directly the situation was totally unacceptable. They would be silenced, and scared to death it was assumed.

Clearly, Major Pullman was unfamiliar with Lucy's bio, the part where she had already served prison time in England, when she had met Alice Paul for the first time. So he was surprised when the two women arrived at the police station and demanded to know the charges against them. Disorderly conduct? No, they just stood there. Inciting to riot? They were just two quiet ladies; they never did riots. Hours passed until they were informed that they had been "obstructing traffic on Pennsylvania Avenue," So there, and not easy to do while juggling a banner.

Lucy and Katherine were dismissed. Next day, June 23rd, four women bearing the same banners were

159

arrested for messing up traffic and then dismissed. But the June 26th arrest of six more Sentinels marked the end of tolerance. These women were tried and found guilty of violating Section Five of the District's Peace and Order Act. Among other strictures which made their behavior a crime was to "…engage in loud or boisterous talking or other disorderly conduct, or to insult or make rude or obscene gestures or comments or observations on people passing, or in their hearing, or to crowd, obstruct or incommode the free use of any street.[68] Somehow they thought it was the unruly crowd that had committed that particular crime.

"Not a dollar of your fine shall we pay," was the answer of the women. "To pay a fine would be an admission of guilt. We are innocent."[69]

The judge was adamant, blaming the women as "the proximate cause of this idle, curious crowd." They would be imprisoned: Katherine Morey, Annie Arneil, Mabel Vernon, Lavinia Dock, Maud Jamison and Virginia Arnold are enshrined in history as the first women to be imprisoned for the right of women to vote. For their "crime," they received a three-day sentence.

The Judge Arthur R. Mullowney, a Wilson appointee, had just experienced his first encounter with the women he would soon grow to detest and victimize. With time, he got better at being mean, because the women left jail after only two days. They returned to a fabulous reception in the walled garden of the Cameron House where a crowd of supporters were gathered and

[68] *Suffragist*, June 30, 1917
[69] Stevens, ed. O'Hare, p.77

they feasted on a sumptuous breakfast of raspberries and cream, bacon, creamed eggs, hot rolls and coffee.

But reaction to the bold Russian Banner caper was mixed. Aware of the British Suffragette' "Get out of Jail Card," i.e. the hunger strike, the *New York Times* commented " Militants Get 3 Days ; Lack Time to Starve[70]. For better or worse, that particular situation was soon to be addressed.

NASWA's duo, Shaw and Catt, who constantly supported Wilson's lack of support, were jealous of the attention the NWP garnered by its upfront tactics. Shaw: "The greatest obstacle now existing." Catt: "Unwise, unpatriotic and unprofitable to the cause of suffrage."[71] And besides they just couldn't stand Alice and Lucy. All they could see was a pair of annoying "young upstarts." But a note arrived, "Congratulations. Stick to it." It was signed *William Parker*, a loyal supporter still in love with Alice.

---

[70] *New York Times*, 18 June 1917
[71] *Bismarck Tribune*, 30 June 1917

---

# Chapter 22

## Truth vs. Power, The Kaiser Banner

Turns out, much to everyone's surprise, including her own, Alice was not invincible. She had reduced the vigil days to once a week and planned each vigil to celebrate a special occasion. The July 4th event went well, the Sentinels' banner celebrated the Declaration of Independence's admonition that "Governments Derive their just powers from the Consent of the Governed." Same old, same old, big response from spectators and police, 18 suffragists arrested, summary trial, three days in jail. Good publicity, suffrage still front and center.

Alice was planning the July 14, Bastille Day event and then she collapsed.

Her furious and unrelenting work schedule and the residual harm from the British force feeding incidents brought about a false diagnosis of Bright's Disease. The "cure" colonic irrigation and static, a treatment involving electricity, didn't kill her, so she was able to direct a planning meeting from her bedside on July 13; Lucy Burns was chosen as acting chair. Treatment at the Quaker institution, Johns Hopkins, in Baltimore, negated the deadly Bright's Disease diagnosis, but mandated a two-month rest period. Alice rested, sort of. William Parker, weighed in with his regrets of not lingering the last he'd seen her. "Of course had I known you were really in need of a word or hand you would have had them."[72] It wouldn't have taken much for Alice to reach out for that hand, but above all, Alice was married to her cause, no time for romance, William, and when mostly rested she would pick up her cudgels again.

So Alice missed the Sentinels storming of the White House on Bastille Day. "Casualties" were many; sixteen in all, among them Alison Hopkins, wife of the man who had convinced Wilson to admit that women were crucial to the war effort. Also Dudley Field Malone, a recent NWP supporter who had been enticed to join the party by Doris Stevens, with whom he was carrying on an illicit love affair. Annoyed at the eloquent defense from Elizabeth Rogers, Mullowney threw the book at the ladies, claiming they used their sex and privilege to avoid consequences after clearly breaking the law. They had obstructed traffic. Such an egregious offense warranted appropriate punishment. The usual $25 fine or 60 days in the Occoquan Workhouse was his considered judgement.

The women were aghast at the thought of two months in a workhouse, but nevertheless, all opted for the wildly inappropriate prison term. Doris Stevens commented, "Now for the first time, I believe, our form

---

[72] Parker to AP

of agitation began to seem a little more respectable than the Administration's handling of it. But the administration did not yet realize this."[73]

J.A.H. Hopkins did and so did Dudley Malone. Immediately they registered their objections with the President. Dudley Malone's concerns included his paramour Doris.

Hopkins had inside knowledge of Wilson's involvement in the arrests, though Wilson had disclaimed any personal involvement. The men prevailed and three days into their sentence, the President pardoned the Occoquan Workhouse prisoners.

Everyone knew that nothing short of the Anthony Amendment's passage would stop the Silent Sentinels but Wilson was dragging his feet; Doris Stevens' sentiments were clear.

We did not regard Mr. Wilson as our president. Since we had no vote we felt he had neither political nor moral claim to our allegiance. ...Here we were a band of women fighting with banners in the midst of a world armed to the teeth...so it is not very difficult to understand how the women grew more resentful of a president's hypocrisy. ...The President's constant oratory on freedom and democracy moved us to scorn. We decided on a protest so militant as to shock not only the President but the public. [74]

Lucy Burns was running the show. She knew the force was with them, but war news commanded the

73 Stevens, ed. O'Hare, p.85
74 Ibid, p.88

headlines and the President's pardon calmed the press. Lucy wanted center stage again and needed some "hectic ideas" to make that happen. So she pried open a can of worms with a flagrant demonstration on August 10. She marched to the White House gates with a brand new banner calling Wilson "Kaiser," equating him with the German Kaiser, the leader of the enemy, Germany.

KAISER WILSON: HAVE YOU FORGOTTEN HOW YOU SYMPATHIZED WITH THE POOR GERMANS BECAUSE THEY WERE NOT SELFGOVERNED? TWO MILLION AMERICAN WOMEN ARE NOT SELF-GOVERNED—TAKE THE BEAM OUT OF YOUR OWN EYE.

Nothing could have caused more trouble. Press reaction was horrendous. Rage turned on the Women's Party. On August 14, a mob descended on the Cameron House, three sailors procured a ladder and climbed the balcony to tear down the Kaiser banners. A bullet crashed into a second floor window and though police finally dispersed the mob, women's banners were again destroyed when they later ventured outside.

One brave soul continued to protest. With no police protection available, next day a frail, barely recovered Alice Paul made her way across Lafayette Square to the White House gates. An angry crowd awaited and immediately swung into action destroying banners and tearing off sashes and clothing too. Alice was thrown three times to the ground.

Finally, after six days of mayhem, the police reacted. They would kill the problem at its source. Free speech, be damned. Major Pullman decreed.

165

Demonstrators, not rioters, would be arrested. On August 17, six women were detained, tried and sentenced to thirty days at the Occoquan Workhouse. While they endured incredible suffering from food laced with worms, forced labor and filthy lack of hygiene, their numbers continued to grow as more women were arrested and sentenced.

Thirty days in the dreaded Occoquan Workhouse had a chilling effect on the Silent Sentinels. Added was the prospect of time spent from home and family obligations. But as the number of incarcerated suffragists grew, Congress grew nervous and in September, the Senate suffrage committee finally issued a favorable report and the House even debated establishing a suffrage committee. Though there were enough Sentinels willing to risk prison, and a spike in donations, Alice had planned to suspend picketing with the October adjournment of Congress. But in early October, Judge Mullowney, with secret knowledge of her plans, suspended sentinels' sentences. Alice then extended the picketing into November, and to amp up the pressure Alice got herself arrested. On October 20 she joined the pickets. Her banner flew high bearing Wilson's bold words. "The time has come to conquer or submit. For us there can be but one choice." She would speak to President Wilson from the pulpit of a prison cell.

# Chapter 23

## "The time has come to conquer or submit"

Either/or.   It was routine now. Pickets parade; pickets arrested no matter their message. Mullowney fixed Alice, "the ringleader" with a sentence longer than anyone else's. She'd get seven months in jail. Alice knew prison; she'd spent enough time in jail to know what to expect.  With grim humor she "relieved" her mother's fears. Her quick note commented that "It will merely be a delightful rest."

Hardly, Alice. Conditions were atrocious. Stench billowed up from each cell's open toilets, especially at night when all windows were shut "Huge rats scrampered [sic] about." another woman found her bed "black with bed bugs," and the rats kept her up at night, making such a noise fighting each other."[75]

More honestly, she confided to Doris Stevens, "However gaily you start out in prison to keep up a rebellious protest, it is nevertheless a terribly difficult thing to do in the face of the constant cold and hunger or undernourishment."[76]

---

[75] Lewis Affidavit, 28 November 19
[76] Stevens,ed. O'Hare, *Jailed* , 114

But, what better strategy than exposing the inhumanity of those persons, her jailers, who were the standard bearers of a repressive government. Public sympathy rests with the oppressed; she'd learned that in England. She would fight to expose unjust circumstances, those planted deeply in skewed righteousness. Her unplanned opportunity arrived with a simple appeal for fresh air. Having been attacked for holding open a window, angry guards carried her to her cell. Then, Alice reverted to her Holloway tactics and pretty soon all the women were breaking their windows with anything handy.

Just before the matrons reluctantly opened some windows, Alice was placed in solitary confinement. Day and night, she was locked in, deprived of mail or visitors or exercise.

Though the jailed suffragists maintained their morale with music from some improvised instruments, nothing could compensate for the rotten meals. Officials figured swill was good enough for miscreants. Raw salted pork sporting an occasional worm was revolting though Lucy Branham, several weeks into her sentence, advised the arrivals how to eat, "Shut your eyes tight, close your mouth over the pork and swallow it without chewing." Alice stuck to the bread, and lost weight and her stamina.

After two weeks, a batch of suffragists, including Lucy Burns, had completed their terms and were released. The seven remaining prisoners were freed from solitary confinement and allowed into the yard. Rose Winslow, a Polish immigrant suffragist, fainted immediately. Alice was too weak to leave her bed. That afternoon both women were confined to the prison hospital. Fresh milk and eggs were offered as hospital fare. Both women refused the food offered. They would not eat well until all prisoners were well fed.

That was when, sharing a room, Alice and Rose decided on "The strongest weapon left with which to continue within the prison our battle against the Administration." The weapon of choice, the trusty old hunger strike guaranteed to embarrass the President.

Alice had to know full well the ordeal she faced. She would be reliving her brutal British experience, but she saw this extreme measure as the most effective way to embarrass the administration since prison officials were agents of the government. It had to have been with extreme trepidation, that Alice made her decision; she would refuse all food.   Rose Winslow likewise.

Immediately, when the women announced their hunger strike, a policy of intimidation ground into gear. Dr. J.A. Gannon's (Bad Doc) sadism was countered somewhat by the presence of Dr. Cora Smith King, (Good Doc) a suffragist sympathizer who managed to secretly act as a go-between, so that Alice could continue to organize her supporters from her hospital bed.

Newspapers picked up the Hunger Strike and so Dr. Gannon devised a plan. Alice would be declared insane and dumped into an asylum, St. Elizabeth's. There she should rot. He sent in Dr. White, who ran St. Elizabeth. The plan was to goad Alice into a heated condemnation of President Wilson.  Though already three days without food, Alice immediately launched into a detailed lecture for the Doctor on her vision for women's rights.

Doctor White was on a mission; he was intent on ferreting out resentment of President Wilson. He interrupted "But hasn't President Wilson treated you women very badly?" Alice, unlike the President, held no personal grudge. She quietly explained that she opposed the President because he held the power to effect suffrage and opposed it. White tried harder. "You are suffering now because of his brutality, are you not?"

Alice's steely eyed vision dealt with facts, not conjecture. "Again I explained it was impossible for us to know whether President Wilson was acquainted in any detail with the facts of our present condition...[77] Then suddenly a light dawned on Alice, Dr. White didn't care a fig about suffrage ; he was looking to prove Alice had an obsession in the face of Wilson's intolerable acts of aggression. If he found a persecution mania, he could declare her insane!

Next day he returned with District Commissioner Gardiner who promised to investigate the horrendous prison conditions if she would give up the hunger strike. Alice countered. Her terms, that the women would be treated as political prisoners, not law breakers for "obstructing traffic."

"Go ahead, force feed her," was his following order to Dr. Gannon. The doctor must have known the horrors of forced feeding[78]. He just hated Alice Paul

---

[77] Stevens, ed. O'Hare, p. 116

[78] Rose Winslow *"Hungry for the Vote"* *Awesome Stories Force Feeding*

that much.  Though Rose Winslow, refused food also, it was Alice who was his nemesis.

## Alice, the Indomitable

Maybe Gannon already knew Dr. White's assessment of Alice's mental state. Alice averred "He," (Dr. White) "wouldn't have anything to do with it. He wouldn't in any way have me transferred to St. Elizabeth.... So I had the greatest determine of indebtedness to him.  And so I am afraid [I might have stayed there forever...][79] Since he couldn't pawn her off to a mental institution, the best Dr. Gannon could do was to place Alice in the prison's psychiatric ward.

Gannon fumed and embellished his Plan B.  He boarded up all her windows, and installed an iron gate on her room. Thrice daily, tubes were thrust into her mouth or nose.

She would not starve on Dr. Gannon's time, and furthermore, in order to "observe her" he had a nurse shine a light on her face every hour. "All through the day and night, once every hour she came in, turned on an electric light sharp in my face, and "observed" me. This ordeal was most terrible torture as it prevented my sleeping for more than a few minutes at a time. If I did finally get to sleep it was only to be shocked immediately into wide-awakeness with the pitiless light. [80]

This practice prevented sleep but did allow her to hear the constant screams of the other psychiatric ward's residents. In the face of these intolerable trials,

---

[79] Fry, Conversations with Alice Paul, p. 199
[80] Stevens ed. O'Hare,  p. 117

Alice dipped into her reservoir of mental resources. With superb mind control she shaped the prisoners' shrieks into sounds from an elevated train. The hourly light flashes were simply met with steely endurance, her innate quality. But who knows how long Alice's mental state could endure? Would Gannon's torture finally have had a broken Alice declared insane? Would he fulfill his vow to destroy her?

Miraculously, after a week, on Nov 13 blessed relief appeared behind the iron gates of her room where Lawyer Dudley Field Malone stood waiting. He had been allowed a visit with the prisoner only upon his threat of a law suit. Alice was ecstatic and after a ninety-minute talk, Malone emerged and confronted Warden Zinkhan with a choice. He might either grant the prisoners recognition as political prisoners or "be discredited as a fool before the whole country."

The next day a stretcher arrived at her iron gate, and Alice was returned to the hospital ward. Though she was still a common "criminal," force fed three times daily, she was freed from the horrors of the psychiatric ward. Sometimes now, a sympathetic nurse would even smuggle in notes from Rose, her partner in pain. Likewise, a charwoman, whose name is unfortunately buried in history, faithfully slipped Alice a paper and pencil daily. On entering Miss Paul's room, she would, with comical stealth, first push Miss Paul's bed elaborately against the door, then practically crawl under it and pass from this point of concealment the coveted paper and pencil. Faithfully every evening, this silent messenger made her long journey after her day's work, and patiently waited while I wrote an answering note to be delivered to Miss Paul the following morning. [81]

Thus it was that indomitable Alice, in a hospital bed, on a hunger strike, and forcibly fed three times daily, with the brave charwoman's help continued to direct the suffragist campaign.

Rose Winslow said it all. "All the officers here know we are making this hunger strike that women fighting for liberty may be considered political prisoners; we have told them. God knows we don't want other women ever to have to do this ever again."[82]

Word about the prison conditions was leaking out and President Wilson could no longer plead ignorance. On November 9th he ordered an investigation which in effect put the cat in charge of the canary. He appointed District Commissioner Gardiner, to determine the treatment of prisoners. Did Gardiner simply not try to verify the prison officials' statements of good order and humane care, or did he simply misrepresent the facts? In either case Wilson could feel comfortable that the women were receiving fit punishment for their crimes of obstructing traffic. "An extraordinary amount of lying," has occurred, he declared.     denying any "real harshness in the treatment."

Rose Winslow's smuggled report saw it differently, but with his conviction providing a clear

---

[81] Stevens, p.98

[82] *The Suffragist Prison, Notes of Rose Winslow* November, 1917

173

conscience, President Wilson was free to take daily
rides and attend the theatre twice weekly.

But unfortunately for the president, since it
became harder and harder for Wilson to ignore the cries
of imprisoned women;  he might have to consider
interrupting  his golf game.

_____

# Chapter 24

# The "Night of Terror" November 14, 1917

Even before she went to prison, Alice realized that with the distraction of the war effort and the sameness of the suffragists' daily presence, her picketing ploy was losing its impact on the both the president and the press. Since it was crucial to keep suffrage front and center in the public eye, she asked herself, "What to do?" and the answer came back, "Swamp the courts with 'lawbreakers'." There was no way at that moment could she have known the nightmare she would unleash.

Dora Lewis, head honcho with Alice in jail, agreed and sent out a call for the biggest picket brigade ever, and they came and marched at the White House. On Saturday, November 10th, forty-one picketers were arrested on the same old, same old. They were, as usual, obstructing traffic, though often the streets were empty. Judge Mullowney, short on prison space, and concerned about the bad publicity for Wilson, let the women post bail and go home. But not until he had lectured them on the enormity of their obstructing traffic offense.

Then when fifty more pickets arrived from all over the country on Sunday, they managed to call to Alice from outside her prison window. Alice responded. For this infraction of prison protocol Alice was punished severely.

On Monday her supporters picketed the White House. As usual, they were arrested and brought before Judge Mullowney. For six interminable hours he sizzled in his seat and pondered the women's fate. Then abruptly, he sent them home again.

The next day they picketed the White House and were arrested and brought before Judge Mullowney who was by then terribly stymied and fresh out of patience. These pesky women were a constant pain in the judge's anatomy and so, exasperated, he told them disappear. He'd call them back when he came up with a good idea.

Immediately the suffragists reconvened at headquarters, the Cameron House, adjusted their hats, unrolled their banners and then, all twenty-seven, plus four more enthusiasts, proceeded in a line to picket the White House. The crowd was unruly and aggressive and they knew they were in for trouble, but had no notion of the amount of sheer hatred and brutality they faced ahead. They were arrested and trucked off to the District Court and spent the night on mats in the District House of Detention. They might have been encouraged if they knew that on the very same day, November 13, Alice, in District Jail, was released from the psychiatric ward. But all they knew was Mullowney being mean.

The irate judge handed out sentences like assorted jelly beans. Alright he showed compassion to 73- year- old Mary Nolan, up from Florida to protest. She got six days, and most only received 15-30 days, but he threw the book at familiar faces. Eunice Brannon and Dora Lewis were sentenced to 60 days. The "Ringleader" the infamous redhead, Lucy Burns, should rot in jail for half a year.

The game plan was to dump the suffragists into district jail along with Alice, their partner in crime, but instead at 5 pm they were herded in the dark on board the south bound train to Virginia, with a stop at Occoquan, the infamous workhouse. Mullowney would have the last say. So at least he thought.

But when the same picketers arrived at Occoquan, all the suppressed furies of Warden R. Whittaker burst on that night of November 14, 1917 as he unwittingly trapped himself in Alice Paul's scheme. The women demanded to be treated as political prisoners, and if denied they would refuse to eat food or to do prison labor. The plan being that because they had come from many different states, the various states' presses would spread their story throughout the country. The administration would be embarrassed, the women released and their suffrage cause greatly strengthened.

Meanwhile on the way to the plan's execution, the women were treated like animals. Doris Stevens remembered.

It was about half past seven at night when we got to Occoquan workhouse. Mrs. Lawrence Lewis, who spoke for all of us, said she must speak to Whittaker, the superintendent of the place…Suddenly the door literally burst open and Whittaker flew in like a tornado; some men followed him…she had hardly spoke up saying we demanded to be treated like political prisoners, when Whittaker said, "You shut up. I have men here to handle you." Then he shouted,

"Seize her!" I saw men spring toward her and then someone screamed, "They have taken Mrs. Lewis!"[83]

"Take that woman," was Whittaker's repeated order, his white hair standing, tiny eyes gleaming, his purple birthmark glowing with sweat. The room filled with men, carrying clubs. One dragged activist Dorothy Day and thinking she was resisting, three guards leaped on her. "My feet were completely off the floor, my arms and shoulders were almost twisted out of joint. One man had his hand at my throat."[84]

Typically, women prisoners were housed in a dormitory, but Whittaker found yet another way to humiliate these upstart suffragists. The guards dragged them to the men's prison and threw them into the stinking cells reserved for crazed convicts. Katherine Lincoln, hurled into a cell. looked across the corridor and offered Eunice Brannan a small smile of consolation. But "Mr. W. suddenly appears wild with fury, his fists clenched. Abuse rains from his crooked mouth and ends with 'or I'll gag you and put you in a straightjacket for the night. Now get away from that door."[85]

All night women huddled three and four to a cell, generally with one bed and one filthy blanket, an open toilet and no privacy. The November night was cold in Occoquan; the women often lay curled on the prison floors.

---

[83] *Jailed* p.123
[84] Affidavit of Dorothy Day, Nov. 28 National Women's Party Papers
[85] Affidavit of Katherine Lincoln Nov. 28 NWPP

---

Whittaker finally left the men's prison to return to the room where he had locked Dora Lewis, the main object of his hatred. "Are you going to give your name or not" raising his arm and clenching his fist. "If you don't, I will put you where the others are." Dora had previously refused to identify herself and she simply shook her head, no. "I was lifted from my chair and dragged down the corridor through the reception room out into the night."[86]

Lucy was frightened for her suffragist sisters and called out their names from her cell. One by one she asked for them until Whittaker arrived, red faced, purple and bright with fury. Lucy didn't stop calling for her comrades. A guard took handcuffs, pulled her arms through the bars and chained her arms high above her head. So she hung for hours, until with Whittaker finally gone, a kinder guard released her. Lucy's buddy, brave Julia Emory raised her fists in sympathy and kept them there till Lucy was cut down.

Likewise, in accordance with Alice Paul's hunger strike in the district jail, on the following days, Dorothy Day and 15 of the jailed women refused to eat and drink the nightly meal of hot milk and fragrant toast served to their cells. Each night rats came to consume the uneaten food as the strikers grew weaker and weaker. Their days devolved into an alternate universe of failing bodies consumed with nausea and fever and fainting. Every possible lie was used to dissuade them from their resolve. To further disorient them their cells were switched almost daily. Outside communication was not allowed and they were told that no one in the

---

[86] Affidavit of Dora Lewis 28 November NWPP

outside knew of their sacrifice and furthermore, the others were eating their food. They persisted. He'd get even. He'd force the hunger strikers to eat.

Elizabeth McShane, a former school principal, described the process. A doctor poured a deadly potion of cold milk and raw eggs into a tube then thrust it into her throat. "Of course a stomach that has been unaccustomed to food for a week cannot take so much liquid cold, all in half a minute…. half through it began to come up, out of the corners of my mouth and down my neck until my hair was stiff with it." When the doctor pulled out the tube, the undigested food followed and covered Elizabeth. Finished with their duty, the doctor and the nurse left her to sit in her vomit.

Though he was an equal opportunity force feeder, Warden Whittaker bore a special animus towards Dora Lewis and Lucy Burns. They were seven days into their hunger strike and he feared that they would up and die on him, causing much embarrassment. He removed them from Occoquan and delivered the women to district jail and into the tender mercies of the merciless Dr. Gannon.

Intrepid Lucy managed to smuggle out notes on little scraps of paper detailing her ordeal. "Doctor Gannon told me then I must be fed. …Whittaker in hall. I was held down by five people at legs, arms and head. I refused to open mouth. Gannon pushed tube up left nostril. I turned and twisted my head all I could, but he managed to push it up. …Tube drawn out covered with blood. Operation leaves one very sick. Food dumped directly into stomach feels like a ball. [87]

The women, Lucy and Dora Lewis, were delivered to the hospital in an ambulance. Next morning the doctor appeared with his handy feeding tube at the ready. "Mrs. Lewis and I said we would not be forcibly fed. Said he would call in men guards and force us to submit. Went away and we were not fed at all this morning. We hear them outside cracking eggs."[88]

Clearly the sounds reverberating outside the jail were louder than eggshells cracking. Word of the sadistic treatment imposed on the women whose crime was "obstructing traffic" had leaked out to the national press just as Alice had predicted. It even reached President Wilson. Concerned for his image, he responded to a NAWSA letter:

> I think our present reply ought to be to the effect that no real harshness of method is being used, these ladies submitting to the artificial feeding without resistance; that conditions…are being investigated for the second or third time but [no abuse] has as yet been disclosed. There being an extraordinary amount of lying about the thing…They offended against an ordinance of the District and are undergoing the punishment appropriate in the circumstances.

Did the president really believe what he said? Did he really feel the newspaper reports were fake news? That's unlikely. He wasn't a sadist, he was just

---

87 Stevens, p.90
88 Ibid p.90

181

frightened by the issue at hand...women were questioning and reacting to their subservient place in society. So maybe he thought that if he played enough golf it would all just go away.

## *Lagniappe: Occoquan Workhouse*

The Occoquan Workhouse was founded in the summer of 1910 with the very best Progressive Era hope that an open air environment and hard work would combine to promote lasting lifestyle reforms for men who were habitual drunks, vagrants and family abusers. The notion was that the men would gain self-esteem and satisfaction by building their own dormitories from lumber forested and bricks created on the site. No cells, no locks, no bars, they were free to work in the surrounding fields and orchard, and so to produce their own food and an additional sense of accomplishment.

So that women could share in this enlightened experiment, the Women's Workhouse was opened in 1912. Those who had been convicted of such crimes as prostitution, disorderly conduct, or drunkenness would receive short sentences. These women contributed by making the clothes for the entire prison population (everyone sewed then), doing the laundry and working in the kitchen.

Somehow the well intentioned ideals of fresh air and fair treatment had dissolved in the years between 1912 and 1917, when the infamous Warden Whittaker took control. Occoquan just descended into a hellhole, its lofty purpose buried in decay and decadence. Ultimately, the Men's and Women's Workhouses were officially closed in 1968.

Today the original homemade brick buildings host a spacious not-for-profit arts center repurposing the liberating intent of its founders. Workhousemuseums.org offers a comprehensive insight into the history and current status of the Workhouse Prison Museum, and offers a virtual tour of the site waiting for the formal opening of the Lucy Burns Museum.

Occoquan Workhouse Exterior (Between 1905-1945) LC DIG-hec-20472

# Chapter 25

## Justice's Wheels Grind…Slowly

Meanwhile back at the workhouse, Lawyer Matthew O'Brien was maneuvering for the suffering suffragists' release. He planned to bring a writ of Habeas Corpus against Warden Whittaker. This writ would insure the right of a citizen to obtain a writ of Habeas Corpus as a protection against illegal imprisonment. His argument was that since the women's "crime" had been committed in the district, they should have been incarcerated in a district jail. Instead they had been confined in Virginia. Clearly, the administration favored Occoquan so as to separate the suffragists from the inspiration of their stalwart leaders in district jail. Best they should all suffer separately.

Anna Shaw and Carrie Chapman Catt embarrassed by the jailed suffragists' loud public sympathy, continued to support President Wilson's righteousness. Shaw commented publicly that "they refuse to eat the food and then they say they are starving." Furthermore she wrote " in my opinion the government has been more mistreated in this whole matter than the pickets, and especially the president of the United States, who has been most patient and courteous."[89] With her, anyway.

---

[89] Shaw to Shippen Lewis, 28 November 1917, NWPP

---

Though O'Brien knew a transfer to a district jail was not desirable, the hunger striking women's woeful appearance in court would be a blatant rebuke of Whittaker's control. But he had to somehow serve wily Whittaker with his subpoena.

Six times the warden managed to avoid, O'Brien, but seven was not his lucky number. On the night of November 21, the lawyer called at Whitaker's house and as ever, was informed that the Warden was not at home. Immediately, O'Brien called from a nearby phone to say he would come again the next day. Then quickly he hotfooted it back to the house, caught him and served the subpoena which would require the Warden to testify. Furious, Whittaker had no choice; he would appear in court on November 27.

There were several reasons the trial date was set for November 27. Whittaker hoped in vain to improve the appalling appearance of the nine-day hunger strikers with offers of food. Additionally, the District Jail's force feeding capacity needed to be increased if Whittaker failed. Matthew O'Brien gasped at the sight of the debilitated women and truly feared they could not live five more days. At his insistence, trial was moved up to November 23.

It was a miserable bunch of women who appeared in Alexandria, Virginia court that day, so disoriented they hardly followed proceedings. Doris Stevens set the scene.

No one present can ever forget the tragi-comic scene set enacted in the little Virginia courthouse that cold, dark November morning. There was Judge Waddill... a mild mannered, sweet-voiced Southern gentleman. There was Superintendent Whittaker in his best Sunday clothes which mitigated very little the cruel and nervous demeanor which no one who has ever come under his control will ever forget. His thugs were there, also dressed in their best clothes which only exaggerated their coarse features and their shifty eyes.[90]

The courtroom was packed with suffragists and reporters who gasped audibly as the woeful women appeared. Again eyewitness Stevens recounts the events.

> ...the women, haggard, red-eyed, sick, came to the bar. Some were able to walk to their seats, others were so weak that they had to be stretched out 6n (sic) the wooden benches with coats propped under their heads for pillows. ...Mrs. Brannon collapsed utterly and had to be carried to a couch in an ante-room.[91]

Surveying the dismal scene, O'Brien noted the absence of Lucy Burns and Dora Lewis.

"They are too ill to be brought to court," Whittaker quickly averred

Lawyer Malone was able to ferret out the fact from District Jail Superintendent Zinkhan that because the two women were being force fed and they were unable to appear.

"How many men does it take to hold Miss Burns?" he asked

"Four."

---

[90] Stevens, p. 104
[91] Ibid p.105

187

"Then Your Honor, don't you think if it takes four men to hold Miss Burns to give her forcible feeding, she is strong enough to appear in Court?" [92]

However, past the point of the mistreatment of the suffragists at Occoquan, the truth to be ascertained was the legality of sentencing the women to a prison in Virginia when their "crime" had been committed in D.C. Again, Zinkhan was caught short when he declared the internment at the workhouse was for "humanitarian" purposes.

Malone, smiled and tilted his head. "Were you actuated by humanitarian motives when you sent Mrs. Nolan, a woman of seventy-three years, to the workhouse.?"

…"Mrs. Nolan will you please stand up?"

Slowly, a frail figure, Mrs. Nolan, stood, pale face, snowy white hair, her thin jaw set. The oldest suffragist's pale eyes condemned the embarrassed Zinkhan.

Judge Waddill, heard arguments through the trial, then recessed himself briefly. He emerged from his chamber to render a decision. "…This class of prisoners and number of prisoners should haze (sic) been given special consideration…and they will be remanded to the custody of the Superintendent of the Washington Asylum and Jail."[93]

[92] Gilmore, Inez Haynes, *Up hill with banners flying*,(Penobscott, Maine., Traversity Press,1964) p.290
[93] Stevens, *Jailed* , p.108.

In a curious bit of reasoning, the good judge further stated that since the women were out of Occoquan, and despite the fact he had labelled their treatment "bloodcurdling," it would not be necessary to investigate conditions there. Humanitarianism, it seems, was in all round short supply in the little Virginia courthouse that day.

So that bedraggled bunch of prisoners were removed to District Jail. Those three who were in imminent danger of death were released on parole, hunger striker Eunice Brannan among them. Then on November 26, it was clear, intrepid Alice had once more outwitted the president's administration. With thirty determined women on hunger strike, of whom eight were in a state of almost total collapse, the Administration capitulated. It could not afford to feed thirty women forcibly and risk the social and political consequences; nor could it let thirty women starve themselves to death, and likewise take the consequences. For by this time one thing was clear; the discipline and endurance of the women could not be broken. And so, all the prisoners were unconditionally released on November 27 and November 28th. [94]

Alice, whose food for the past three weeks had been forcibly fed to her, was sprung first. For those who thought she might be suppressed by her ordeal she had this comment. "We hope that no more demonstrations will be necessary, that the amendment will move steadily on to passage and ratification without further

[94] Ibid, p.108.

suffering or sacrifice. But what we do depends entirely upon what the Administration does." [95]

There was a hot time at old Cameron House that night! Lucy Burns had lost thirty pounds. Friends slipped three fingers under Alice's wrist band. Hunger strikes are a dubious choice for weight loss, but a definite source of inflammatory press attention.

No wonder these unbeatable suffragists were then labelled 'Iron Jawed Angels." And the fight hadn't even begun.

---

[95] Ibid p.108

# Chapter 26
## Time out...Misery Delayed

During the trial on November 23, Lucy Burns received word that she had been proposed as a candidate for congress from New York. Fortunately, on November 6, 1917, New York State had just become the first eastern state to grant women the right to vote, so she'd not risk arrest if she voted for herself. She turned down the offer; her heart wanted the Anthony Amendment and universal suffrage. But she did return to Brooklyn to recuperate from her ordeal. Alice, likewise, "rested" at Cameron House for three weeks, nursed back to well-being by the healthy residents.

So they both probably missed President Wilson's speech to congress on December 4. He spoke eloquently as usual, setting forth his opinions on war with Austria, control of water power, railroad legislation and more. He somehow forgot to mention the elephant in the room, the national consciousness of the suffragists ordeal during the "Night of Terror."

But the ladies didn't. Immediately the NWP called a conference for December 6$^{th}$ to 9$^{th.}$ One strategy presented was to bring damage suits totaling a hefty $8000.00 against, among others, Warden Zinkhan and Superintendent Whittaker. "The suits were brought in no spirit of revenge, but merely that the Administration should not be allowed to forget its record of brutality, unless it chose to amend its conduct by passing the Amendment.[96]

Though neither of the above actually happened, the victory party did. The Belasco Theatre was jammed to the rafters and "…there was an overflow meeting of four thousand outside on the sidewalk.…Elsie Hill addressed this overflow meeting which shivered in the bitter cold for over an hour, yet stayed to hear her story."[97]

Inside the theatre hilarious celebration prevailed. There was speechifying and a grateful acknowledgement of the $86,386.00 raised to further the cause. Then, eighty-one women in white, all of whom had served in the jail or the workhouse, carrying lettered purple, white, and gold banners, marched down the two center aisles of the theatre and onto the stage. …On that occasion, prison pins which were tiny replicas in silver of the cell doors, were presented to each "prisoner of freedom."

As Alice Paul appeared to receive her pin, Dudley Field Malone called, "Alice Paul," and the audience leaped to its feet; the cheers and applause resounded until she disappeared at the back of the platform. Post prison Alice finally got around to consoling her long suffering mother. She was comforted in her recovery by the always faithful William Parker, who had stayed on through all of her ordeals, staunchly supporting her. But then, by 1918 it was obvious to him that Alice's first love was her cause and again rejected, William Parker left town and Alice. William never found another love. He never married. Alice was irreplaceable, too tough an act to follow.

---

[96] Stevens, p. 110
[97] Gilmore, p. 298

---

Alice rested in her recovery until she was bolted from her sick bed on word that the new House Representatives were taking a vote on the Suffrage Amendment. The numbers actually looked good. Two thirds of the Republicans were already on board, but she'd need some Democrats to win the vote. With little time to lose, she zeroed in on President Wilson, convinced that his influence would be the deciding factor. Suffragists besieged the White House with urgent pleas for his support. Democrats were reminded that in the upcoming 1918 elections, angry women voters might eliminate their majority.

It arrived not a moment too soon; a vote was scheduled for December 10th 1917 The same women who had picketed and been imprisoned appeared early at the East Gallery doors. Prepared to knit the day long, creating sweaters and socks for the boys fighting in Europe, their "weapons" aka knitting needles were confiscated at the door. No matter, they'd hidden sandwiches; they were in for the long haul.   Shortly, Carrie Chapman Catt and Anna Shaw arrived.

Their contribution to the amendment's passage had largely consisted of agreeing with Wilson's state by state obstruction and just lately advocating for it, a swift philosophical bait and switch. In full sight of the heroic hunger strikers, they were seated in the House Speaker's private gallery. Likewise, some Representatives, e.g. Scott Ferris, Oklahoma Democrat, railing against the suffragists efforts to embarrass the party in power, disavowed the suffragists' behavior as having influenced their votes.

Kentucky Republican John Langley viewed the women through a different lens. "When passing up and down the Avenue I frequently witnessed cultured, intellectual women arrested and dragged off to prison because of their method of giving publicity to what they believed to be the truth."  Clearly Congressman Langley sympathized, but didn't match the ardor of New York Representative Frederick Hicks, Jr. who at her request, left his dying wife to vote for suffrage. Mrs. Hicks, an ardent suffragist died that night.

The House voted once, then a recount was demanded. The East Gallery contingency was chewing its fingernails, not sandwiches when the second vote was called.  One by one the ayes and nays were sounded as the 309 men and 1 woman, Jeanette Rankin, cast their votes.

The House Caves!


Wild cheers erupted as The Anthony Amendment reached the required two thirds majority and passed the Constitutional Amendment 136-274 with not one vote to spare. Singing for joy, in unison, the Battle Hymn of the Republic, embracing and weeping, exactly one year since they'd begun to picket, the Silent Sentinels were noisy and giddy with joy. Lucy, Dora Lewis, Doris Stevens, Maud Younger, Ann Martin celebrated the historic event. They looked about in vain for Alice. She was gone.

Always a step ahead, they found Alice at her desk back in the new Jackson St. house.  Her cryptic comment to the jubilant women placed the suffragists' triumph in context. She knew the battle for women's rights was far from won. "Eleven to win before we can pass the Senate."[98]

No time for a victory lap. With so much else to do, she'd start with a "Prison Special." Women must be recruited to ride the rails countrywide wearing their Occoquan outfits and stirring up support. With characteristic unfailing prescience she knew she must ready her people for the next suffrage wars.

Maybe also, the President feared a tide of newly enfranchised women voting Republican in the now twelve suffrage states. His daughter, a suffrage supporter, might have whispered in his ear. Or maybe it was the adverse public opinion generated by his administration's brutal treatment of those indomitable women, namely Alice Paul and friends. For whatever reason, President Wilson shocked the nation on December 9th when he told a visiting delegation of Democratic Congressmen that the Anthony Amendment was an "act of right and justice." It was hardly a rousing endorsement but one he allowed into the press. Alice waited, scared but hopeful. Was she right in her assessment? Would his support be the clincher?

---

[98] *New York Herald Tribune,* 11 January 1918

# Part Six: The Beginning of the End of the End of the Beginning

## (1918-1920)

## Chapter 27

## Alice Keeps the Home Fires Burning

Alice had done the numbers. A 2/3 majority vote was needed to pass a constitutional amendment through the Senate. Alaska and Hawaii, were absent in 1918, so of the 96 senators, 64 "Ayes" were necessary. On Feb. 15, 1919 she'd start with the Prison Special. Women must be recruited to ride the rails countrywide wearing their Occoquan outfits and colorfully advertising the battle for suffrage raging in the Senate. Aboard the train, garbed in her prison stripes, rode the redoubtable Mary Nolan, 74 now.

And with no rest for the weary, eleven Senators at least must be won over before the 65th Congress would adjourn in March, 1919. Switching tactics for a spell, Alice placed lobbying and the threat of anti-suffrage Democratic defeat in the fall 1918 elections at the forefront. Quickly she aimed the intractable Maud Younger at their wavering heads. Telling of the attitude prevalent in some senators, she approached Senator James Reed, (D. Missouri) His response made for colorful retelling so she copied his fuming, word by word.

"Women don't know anything about politics. Did you ever hear them talking together?" Maud might have assured him that she was a woman, and probably better able than he to comment on female conversation. But amused by his bombast she continued to listen and write. "Well first they talk about fashions and children and housework; and then perhaps— about churches, and then about theatre." His voice rose to a triumphant squeak, "and then about literatoor! Yes, and that's the way it ought to be."[99]

But Maud was undeterred and by mid -June, her band of lobbyists had narrowed the anti-suffragists to just three holdout senators. She had used a lethal lobbying weapon, all her own. It was stored in a spare room in headquarters, a huge filing cabinet and containing detailed information on every member of congress. She knew their whims, their wants, and their work habits. A suffrage sympathizer might just show up at a senator's golf game   Particularly crucial to the trove was the individual congressman's relationship with his mother. Experience had demonstrated that, to quote Maud, "some married men listen more to their mothers, than to their wives."[100]

So close to victory, twice the Senate Suffrage Committee Chairman announced dates for a vote, only to be thwarted by wily antics from the antis. A southern senator's unannounced June 27 filibuster finally doomed the vote for that session, and Alice, discouraged with protocol, reluctantly once more, channeled her inner militant. An imposing, marble statue of the Marquis of Lafayette stood elevated on his three story pedestal within full view of the White House.  That brave

---

[99] Walton, p. 214 Younger *"Revelations, Part 3,"*

[100] Ibid, 217

Frenchman who had defied his times to fight for justice was the perfect foil for the suffragists' message.

For several weeks the authorities had refused permission for any suffrage street meetings, so Alice didn't ask, she just went ahead with plans for the demonstration. She felt sure they wouldn't be arrested since recently their picketing convictions had been declared unlawful. The night of August 5th headquarters at Jackson Place rocked with noisy reunions and celebratory glee as veterans of Occoquan and District Jail hunger strikes mixed with excited newbies thrilled with their first demonstration. Alice taking refuse for the night, camping out on the roof was soon joined by late night party persons. The suffragists' mood was irrepressible. Delighted Alice joined the ebullient women dancing through the night.

Next day, Doris Stevens describes the scene. Nearly one hundred women from many States in the Union, dressed in white, marched from Headquarters to the monument carrying banners of purple, white and gold, led by a standard bearer carrying the American flag. They made a beautiful mass of color as they grouped themselves around the statue. One banner bore Inez Milholland's memorable last words…HOW LONG MUST WOMEN WAIT FOR LIBERTY?

Always dependable, a revived Dora Lewis stepped up to address the crowd. "We are here because our country is at war for liberty and democracy…" Mid-sentence she was grabbed by policemen and, as the viewers stood amazed, she was arrested and dragged off. Hazel Hunkins of Montana immediately stepped forward to take her place. Bravely she spoke, "Here at the statue of Lafayette, who fought for the liberty of this country," A few bold words later she too was shut down. Miss Vivian Pierce, pushed forward but only got so far as "President Wilson has said…" One after another, replacing themselves, the women continued, trying to speak and being arrested. Lavinia Dock, singing loud, didn't get through the first verse of "America" before she was silenced. An officer spied Alice in the crowd and shouted for her arrest also, "That's the leader. Get her!"[101]

Before the crowd could really appreciate what had happened, forty-eight women, had been hustled to the police station by the wagon load, their gay banners floating from the backs of the somber patrol wagons. …All were released on bail and ordered to appear in court the following day.[102]

No rest for the weary police, the irksome women again surrounded the Lafayette statue. Those who hadn't been arrested already showed up on August 12. They were arrested only to be followed by those not already culled by police, by another group on August 14.

Judge Mullowney had quit his job in a snit, annoyed that his perfectly good suffragists' sentences had been declared illegal. His replacement Judge McMahon, looking desperately for an offense with which to charge the women, suspended their sentences claiming he needed time to figure things out. In Congress, Republicans took no time to capitalize on the adverse publicity, calling the Democrats to task for blocking the amendment vote.

Trial of the first group finally took place on August 15. After much deliberation, a charge had been "figured out." Not only had the women been guilty of "holding a meeting in a park," but also had shamelessly committed the egregious offence of "Climbing a Statue." The women, 26 of them, were sentenced to prison for terms of five to fifteen days. They

---

[101] *Suffragist.* 5 "Women's Protest"[106]

[102] Stevens, ed O'Hare, p. 143

would be incarcerated in an abandoned workhouse on the grounds of the District Jail.

The administration clearly had learned little from the Occoquan debacle, but willfully entered into a publicity nightmare. The workhouse building had been declared unfit for human habitation in 1906.

The place was the worst the women had experienced. Hideous aspects which had not been encountered in the workhouse and jail were encountered here. The cells were damp and cold. The doors were partly of solid steel with only a small section of grating, so that a very tiny amount of light penetrated the cells. The cots were of iron, without any spring and with only a thin straw pallet to lie upon. So frightful were the nauseating odors which permeated the place, and so terrible was the drinking water from the disused pipes, that one prisoner after another became violently ill.[103]

Fetid water was running through rusted pipes and ghoulish Dr. Gannon was at it again. All but two elderly women were on a hunger strike, so to retaliate he refused them medical care. District Commissioner Brownlow devised a special form of torture for the hunger strikers. He hired chefs to set up stoves in the corridors to cook a luscious ham, with its delicious fragrance wafting through the dank corridors, he was convinced that the women's resolve would melt.

Once again, the authorities were caught red-handed. Senators demanded to see their jailed constituents and news of the women's treatment spread like disease. Five days later, Wilson returning from "the best rest in years," ordered the women freed. The same day, Alice was granted permission for park demonstrations. Relieved, Alice would continue to use public facilities to state the suffrage case.

---

[103] Stevens, ed O'Hare, p.144

Then there was even more good news. A Republican Caucus had called for an immediate vote on women's suffrage. Dedicated anti-suffragists were eying November's upcoming elections with trepidation. Alice wanted that vote, and for once NASWA agreed. But Alice would do more than cozy up to the President.

Now that she was legal, she'd pull off a bigger, bolder demonstration. Alice figured she'd take it to the limit next time and put some unsuspecting congressional feet to the fire.

# Chapter 28

## A Race to the Deadline - So Close, So Very Close

If Alice Paul had a "to do" list, it might look like the following.

September 16, 1918

- Get W. W's comments to southern and western suffragist delegation at 2:00 pm today. Copy the part where he said "…I have endeavored to assist you in every way in my power, and I shall continue to do so. I will continue to do so. I will do all I can do to urge the passage of the amendment by an early vote."

- Talk to Doris Stevens who should immediately go to Senators Overman and Jones to see if W.W.'s statement has changed their minds, since they would be the deciding votes.

- Tell the crowd of suffragists ready to march that Doris said, "These administration leaders said that…the President's statement did not mean that a vote would be taken this session…Such a situation was intolerable. The President was uttering more fine words, while his Administration leaders interpreted them to mean nothing."[104], but they were not followed by action on his part.

- Buy a sturdy urn, suitable for burning speeches. Buy matches to light up the torches (it might be dark by 6 o'clock) Finish sewing banners, make LOTS of banners, the purple, white and gold kind. All these new young women want to carry banners.

- Tell William Parker I'm sorry. And good-bye

---

[104] Stevens ed. O'Hare, p.146.

With drama designed specifically to catch the public's attention, the suffragists stepped out into the late afternoon, on September 16. The long, white line proceeded to Lafayette Square where as the procession assembled, beautiful young Lucy Branham, stepped forward to address the assembled crowd. "The torch which I hold symbolizes the burning indignation of the women who for years have been given words without action…We have protested to this administration by banners; we have protested by speeches; now we protest by this symbolic act…by consigning their hollow phrases to the flames."[105]

That which didn't kill Lucy Branham, the rotted pork dinners at Occoquan, and solitary confinement there, had made her strong. Her words rang through the night as she deliberately took her torch to the President's words and dropped the flaming papers into the urn waiting at Lafayette's statue's foot.

The demonstrators braced themselves for the usual onslaught, but somehow a miracle had occurred. Instead of physical attacks they were showered with money! It began when one man handed up a $20. bill. Then more came and even more. Eye witness Doris Stevens recounted the scene. "Instantly marshals ran hither and thither collecting the money in improvised baskets while the cheers grew louder and louder."

Wilson heard the roars as he stepped out for his afternoon drive. He rerouted his limo, but couldn't escape its message. Despite his "powerless" claim, the next day, the Chairman of the Senate Suffrage Committee placed vote on the Anthony Amendment on the agenda for September 26.

---

[105] Ibid p.148

## Finally, Woodrow

They might have seen the outcome of that initiative. Much debate ensued, and ensued, and ensued for hours, and days on end. Then on September 30 as the Senate issued a collective gasp, President Wilson swept into the chamber, accompanied by his wife, Edith, and her mother and sister. He knew his party was in jeopardy as was his world vision to promote democracy abroad, given that at home he opposed democracy for women. Ever articulate, the President pleaded his so very newly found cause, the value of women's participation. "We shall need their moral sense to preserve what is right and fine and worthy in our system of life as well as to discover just what it is that ought to be purified and reformed.

Without their counsel we will surely be half-wise."[106] Evidently the Senate majority chose to be halfwits, since they would continue to exclude women from true democracy. On October 1, The Anthony Amendment was defeated, just two small votes from Senate passage

Alice wouldn't get mad. She'd get even.

---

[106] Stevens, ed O'Hare, *Jailed* , 152

# Chapter 29
## Wilson Gets Burned...in Effigy

For a minute Alice doubted herself. Maybe she did need more than Wilson's support. And to make matters worse, the 65th Congress would end its term in March, 1919, at which point, unless the Amendment had been passed, it would have to be considered and approved by both houses all over again.

For one thing she and the rest of the country needed relief from the flu epidemic which raged.

World War I claimed an estimated 16 million lives. The influenza epidemic that swept the world in 1918 killed an estimated 50 million people. One fifth of the world's population was attacked by this deadly virus. Within months, it had killed more people than any other illness in recorded history.[107]

Alice was too busy to be sick. Suffragists, despite the challenges of health and opposition from guards, continued to picket the Capitol and advocate for the pro suffrage candidates nationwide. The vote on November 5 produced a Republican win, and almost insured Amendment passage in the 66th Congress. Great news! Even greater news!  The War in Europe, WW1 ended on November 11, 1918 but with the general euphoria, suffrage and the Anthony Amendment were

---

[107] Archives.gov/exhibits/influenza-epidemic

buried. Alice had to think hard and fast to keep Votes for Women, a national priority.

Events started coming quickly. There was no time to lose. Mid December, the 16th and the anniversary of the Boston Tea Party, 300 women marched to Lafayette Square to burn Wilson's speeches and pronouncements in a flaming protest. America noticed, but the President's attention was elsewhere.

He and Edith had embarked on a two-month European mission to enact his dream of a world body dedicated to peace and wellbeing, the proposed League of Nations.

For the third year, Alice would skip Christmas at home in Paulsdale, Tacie resigned to her absence, though probably immensely proud of her valiant daughter, would mail her gift. Around the comforts of a big fire, Alice and cohorts would hatch their plans for 1919. Had he known, the President might have been uncomfortable about the events on the calendar back home in D.C. Sound and fury would reign on New Year' Day.

January 1, 1919, saw Dora Lewis and others diligently light a small urn at their customary White House picketing spot as the brand new bell at headquarters tolled support across the square. But Alice's plan for a perpetual "Watchfire for Freedom" at the White House was short-lived. A banner was unfurled accusing the absent president of "deceiving the world when he appears as the prophet of democracy."[108]

These words were red flags to service men loyal to their Commander-in-Chief. Dora tried to explain but several rushed forth, knocking down women and overturning the urn and dousing the fire. Watching from across the way in the park, Alice, who expected trouble, simply lit her emergency second urn.

---

[108] *Suffragist* Jan 11, 1919

More Watchfires, tended by dedicated suffragists, burned on, day and night, until January 4th when the police reverted to arresting women. Over three days, they arrested 11 women, including Alice, for the quickly invented crime of "lighting fires after sundown in a park." They were sentenced to five to ten days in the District Jail, cleaned up now, but still run by sadistic Warden Zinkhan. Immediately the prisoners declared a hunger strike, passing time with songs and stories and the observation of the living habits of cockroaches and rats.[109] Alice dashed off a note to her mother, with the words no mother wanted to hear. "Was sentenced to prison for five days, so cannot see you tomorrow. Sorry to miss you."[110] Tacie and Helen came anyway. Zinkhan barred their visit.

With Alice in jail, Lucy Burns and Mabel Vernon assumed charge of the Watchfires and now set a fire for each time Wilson spoke from Europe. Relentlessly, the clock continued to count down to March 3rd, the final day of the 65th Congress. With no Senate affirmative vote by then, the issue would need to be reintroduced and reaffirmed by yet another vote in the House. Alice was desperate for the crucial Senate vote and recruited members to urge for the state resolutions which would sway the senators.

### The Ultimate Indignity:

### Burning the President in Effigy

Fortunately, Alice was released now, and with little time remaining before Senate adjournment, and only one vote blocking passage, Alice planned the mother of all dramatic demonstrations for the night before the February 10th crucial Senate vote on the Anthony Amendment. She would enact the ultimate insult to the seemingly hypocritical President, preaching for democracy abroad in Europe, while not truly

---

[109] ibid
[110] Walton, p.231

supportive at home. On that night the President's likeness would be burned in effigy.

And, so into the evening's gloom with a bell tolling unceasingly from the upper floor of headquarters, the doors opened and a line of 100 women bearing bright anti-Wilson banners stepped out. Next to appear, two sturdy young, women carrying aloft the Watchfire for Freedom Urn, and then finally in the procession, 26 suffragists marched behind ready to burn their sheaves of wood.

The mood was quiet, intense; the task was dangerous This would be no ordinary Watchfire vigil, this was the night of their most outrageous act. Burning the president's likeness in effigy might finally inflame some Anthony Amendment passion on the part of the ambivalent ultimate Democratic deciding vote.

The police closed in as the president's portrait was dropped into the cauldron, and instantly the law's heavy hand fell. Indiscriminate arrests followed. Women with banners were taken; women without banners were taken. Women attempting to guard the fire; women standing by doing nothing at all; all were seized and rushed to the patrol…When the patrol wagons were all filled to capacity nearby automobiles were commandeered and more patrols summoned."[116]

Then, suddenly the police stopped their arrests. Their jail, already overcrowded, simply could not accommodate any more miscreants. For another hour the women guarded the burning Watchfire, then finally, as the night darkened, the sixty remaining protestors returned to headquarters marching to the cadence of the tolling bell. Thirty-nine protesters were missing, arrested. The tolling bell was silenced,

Next day, February 10, by one vote, the Senate rejected the Anthony Amendment. and for all of the dedicated and fearless hunger strikers, picketers and prisoners, the 65th

Congress would shut down on March 4, 1919, with no constitutional amendment barring sexual discrimination in the voting place. suffragists thwarted, the tally was again one vote short of passage.

Alice had every right to give up.

But, undaunted, with only a short time before the 65th Congress concluded in March. Alice immediately launched the formidable Lucy Burns, and the redoubtable Mary Nolan, now 74, and others to tour the country on the "Prison Special," showing lantern slides and sharing their experiences and future hopes with welcoming crowds. Dressed up in their best prison garb, they reenacted their ordeal at Occoquan, thus demonstrating the injustice of denying women the vote.

Wilson, home now from Europe, was followed by determined suffragists, who were duly arrested in Boston, and even brutally attacked outside New York City's Metropolitan Opera House where he was to speak. His words were hardly music to those women enduring the onslaught of furious police, soldiers and even bystanders.

# Chapter 30

## Shove comes to Push, A Chilling Climax and the Ultimate Irony

For all the angst, the pain of hunger strikes, the rat infested jail cells, the years of public scorn, the end came without drama. Republicans anxious to enhance the inevitable, embarrassed Wilson, fresh back from advocating again for democracy in Europe.

By then, suffrage matters were reaching a crisis at home for several reasons: by 1919, 28 states now offered votes for women, suffrage was already almost universal in Europe, cabinet members needed appropriations to pay off their war debts, and politicians wanted to appease women so they would relinquish their wartime jobs to returning veterans. For all of the above, Wilson, pressured by his supporters from across the Atlantic, called a Special Session of Congress. Circumstances assured Senate passage because the two newly elected Democrat senators were beholden to the President. Only one affirmative vote was needed. Wilson summoned Senator William Harris of Georgia, one of the above, who happened to be in Italy at the time, to meet him in Paris. The Senator came, consented and cabled his support.

On May 19, 1919, the 66th Congress convened with a large Republican majority and to no one's surprise, on June 4[nd] the deciding Senate with little fanfare, cemented into law the ridiculously long overdue constitutional guarantee of women's democratic right to vote.

Jubilation reigned at headquarters. Suffragists sang and danced with glee. Congress had finally caved. It was celebration time, a victory party. Unmitigated joy and the culmination of years spent in suffering and turmoil had finally achieved what was a blatantly fundamental right.

As ever, Alice was a no show at the love fest. She was elsewhere, in fact, she was in St. Paul, Minnesota. It was fine to feel good about Congress, but she was well aware that reality lay in the ratification process, and Alice was painfully addressing that fact. It would take money to convince state legislators, and Alice, as ever, was out west scrambling for resources.

Moreover, hunger strikes were passé. If she had to find another way to keep the cause in the national consciousness, why not play the model woman card? She would emulate the historic avatar of women's virtue, and that would be, Betsy Ross. The bold suffragist would douse Watchfires, roll up the banners, and terminate the Prison Special. No more a"militant," Alice appeared on the *Suffragist* cover, dutifully sewing a star for each ratified state. Her intent being that anti-suffragists could be consoled by the fact that though they voted now, women would stay domestic.

Then in October, 1919, Woodrow Wilson suffered an incapacitating stroke and to keep the matter quiet, his wife, Edith Galt, assumed his tasks, albeit de facto, the first woman "President" of the United States.

Though Alice's new ploy had no effect on most southern states, up north, prospects looked better. Wisconsin immediately ratified, narrowly beating out Illinois and Michigan. Now thirty-three more states were needed to reach the "Perfect 36", the three quarter majority necessary for ratification. But even though 22 states had ratified the Anthony Amendment by December, 1919, all the predictable, Democrat controlled states had been counted in, and a harbinger of bad news, already Georgia and Alabama had said no to women's rights. Georgia had high poll taxes and impossible literacy tests to prevent black men from voting, and had no intention of complicating matters with votes for black women.,

The chase for votes was on and stories abound. Lillian Kerr, an NWP worker, reported on the Oklahoma debate "...a terrible ordeal-blood, thunder, riot and sudden death type of argument from our opponents."[111] A hair-raising cross-country $5,000 railroad dash into the deadlocked West Virginia Assembly brought the erstwhile vacationing Senator Bloch home to break the 14-14 state senate tie. In New Jersey, the Liquor Lobby, reacting without mercy to the Prohibition of Alcohol Amendment, almost drowned the vote. An ardent final appeal from Senator Sheldon Spenser, Missouri, charged the moment and changed the vote. In late afternoon, March 10, New Jersey became the 34th state to ratify, then on March 22, a suffrage win in the state of Washington, pushed the count to 35. Alice Paul and her unflinching supporters were just one excruciating yes away from victory.

But from whence might that last vote be wrung? Pickings were getting really slim. Eight southern states had rejected ratification, (though late to the party, Florida did finally ratify the 19th Amendment. In 1969 the Florida legislation passed the Anthony Amendment without the governor's signature.) Alice did the math: 48 states minus the 35 already yes, the 8 rejected, equals 5 possibilities: 2 in New England, with Connecticut and Vermont's anti-suffrage governors refusing to hold special legislative sessions, Louisiana, Tennessee and then there was Delaware. With the 2 southern states, plus 2 immovable objects in New England, Delaware remained her crucial last living hope.

---

[111] Kerr to Paul, 26 February 1920, NWPP

Delaware, was a sure win according to Carrie Chapman Catt. She whose contributions to suffrage had largely been elsewhere, saw Delaware as the 36th vote, and held a "Victory Celebration" even as debate raged, and then promptly left for England. She could have saved her party's money. Delaware, sharing close quarters on the Delmarva Peninsula with Virginia and Maryland, joined those states in rejecting ratification. Slim pickings became no pickings at all.

A most ridiculous option opened though, through the vagaries of a U.S. Supreme Court decision, Tennessee became a most improbable option. Undaunted, unrealistically determined, Alice assessed the situation. An election year, 1920 saw New York Republican Warren Harding pitted against Democrat Governor James Middleton Cox. A suffragist operative bounced back and forth, between their local Tennessee offices, pitting Harding vs Cox, demanding from each man a commitment to support ratification.

It would be necessary to call a special session of the Tennessee Legislature and that summer of 1920, Governor Roberts did not seem so inclined. Maybe it was the heat in Nashville, or maybe the hot whoosh of Woodrow Wilson's telegram from Washington, but Governor Roberts finally did call for a Special Session to convene at noon, on August 9. As pro and antis arrived at the train station, lively activists pinned roses to their lapels: red-ante, yellow-pro. And that pleasant reception was a peaceful beginning to what became a legislative brawl. Not in the State Senate, where on August 13, the vote was 25 ayes to 4 nays, 2 abstentions, but in the House the pro vote was in trouble, and the atmosphere was charged with paranoia and prejudice and not a little skullduggery.

On Monday, the House's first order of business was a motion to adjourn until the following morning, Tuesday August 17. Opposition's 52 to 44 vote boded ill for the suffragists. Meanwhile dirty tricks prevailed as the pro suffrage leader, Joe Hanover received suggestive phone calls in an attempt to compromise the young bachelor on the eve of the big vote. Even worse, more calls threatened his life if he didn't relent his position.

August 18, vote day saw a packed chamber, with crowds waiting outside. The day might live in history, or become yet another tiresome footnote. The galleries were jammed with suffrage supporters, all in white with their traditional yellow sashes gleaming. Red roses adorned antis, including Harry Burn, fresh out of the town of Mouse Creek, Tennessee, and at 24 the youngest legislator. Mouse Creek, a farming community, was overwhelmingly anti-suffrage. They'd sent Harry there to take care of business. His job was to shut down the crazies, but hesitant Harry had his conscience in his pocket.

A day of intense drama and unexpected surprises began at 10:30. First was the last minute defection of House Speaker Seth Walker, whose surprising abrogation of his suffrage support brought a crew of antis with him. Confidant of victory, they voted to table the motion, and deliver a swift death to women's votes.

A roll call to favor tabling the motion would cement the amendment's fate and it began. Harry Burn, red rose blooming, said a confidant "aye." And so it went, each member called his preference, with one exception. Banks Turner, a Democrat, said nothing when he was called. After an awkward silence, he was just listed as an abstention, leaving the final count tally, 48 for tabling, 47 against tabling. Suffrage was dead; yellow roses withered.

Then a voice rose from the floor. It was Banks Turner, suddenly energized. His voice resounded through the shocked galleys "I wish to be recorded as against the motion to table." Amazed Walker quickly contrived a recount but failed to change the numbers. Furious now, Walker moved in for a kill, a flat out vote aye or nay", should put an end to suffrage in Tennessee and by doing so, defeat the Anthony Amendment.

House Members spoke, "Aye, Aye, Nay, Nay, Nay, Nay," then Harry Burn, shaky hand clutching a note in his pocket, voted. With a low, barely audible voice, he said, "Aye," and with that one soft word young Harry Burn, from Mouse Creek, Tennessee, created history.

(Banks Turner, abstained. Now emboldened he voted again. His "Aye," bringing the final count to 49 pros, 47 antis.) So the Anthony Amendment against all odds was passed in Tennessee, by just one word. The event that ushered women into their own constitutional rights had happened. Votes for women was permanent now, 72 long, often dreadful years in the making.

But what exactly was in that letter in Harry Burn's pocket?

It read like this: *Dear Son, Harrah and vote for suffrage. Don't keep them in doubt…Your Mother.* Febb Burn, a widow, with a farm to run and no equal rights, knew injustice first hand. So, in the very last, final analysis, it was a single woman who won Tennessee and suffrage.

Meanwhile back in Washington, Alice Paul and her legion of suffragists, triumphantly toasted the Betsy Ross banner. Stars now numbered the perfect 36. The battle was over. Justice prevailed. Mission accomplished.

Time to move on, Alice

Alice Paul, Raising Glass c.1920 Biog File LC-Dig ds 00180

## Postscript: Take That Alice

Despite the joy of conquest, on the triumphal day of the Anthony Amendment's signing into law, Carrie Chapman Catt stayed bitter and Woodrow Wilson, though debilitated, still managed to spread his ill will toward Alice Paul and her National Women's Party. The *New York Times* edition of Friday, August 27, 1920 reported on all the celebratory suffrage news that was fit to print:

Late this afternoon, Mrs. Carrie Chapman Catt, head of the National American Women's Suffrage Association, and Mrs. Helen Gardiner another active worker in that organization, were received at the White House by President and Mrs. Wilson. The National Women's Party, known as the militants, and a rival organization to that headed by Mrs. Catt, was not represented.

Though Secretary of State Bainbridge Colby, who was to sign the 19th Amendment into law, had stated unequivocally that he would allow no visitors, the Times goes on to say,

Representatives of both factions visited the State Department this morning. Mrs. Catt and members of her party were photographed by movie operations as they left the State Department. Miss Alice Paul and her associates of the militant wing of the suffragists waited in the corridor of the State Department to be seen by the Secretary of State who sent word he would receive them but at this moment the Spanish Ambassador arrived and took precedent over the delegation of militants.

As time wore on the "militant wing" thinned and finally left the department without having an audience with the Secretary of State.

Alice seemed to hold no animosity toward the forces which opposed and often abused her. Both/And" explains her attitude toward the hostile NASWA/Congressional Union split, as she began to flex her organizational muscles. When asked to condemn President Wilson who tolerated her unjust imprisonment and subsequent abuse, she simply presented his reasons for his behavior.

Over and again, biographers look for the wellsprings of Alice Paul's extraordinary mindset. Obviously, her very being reflected the tenets of her Quaker formation, but where did her endless patience and her unshakable calm come from while she was subjected to the most trying and cruel circumstances?

Alice probably was not aware of the teachings of Lao Tzu the legendary founder of Taoism, but somehow she seems to practice its mantra. Her prototype seems almost to be outlined by the definition of a Taoist as set out in Religionfacts.com. "The ideal person in philosophical Taoism is the sage who understands and lives…knowing that all opposites are relative and interdependent".

Another tenet of Tao stresses "non-action". That is not Alice at all, but digging deeper one discovers non-action does not mean no action but actually teaches that "Perfect activity leaves no track behind it." Alice, the genius behind the movement, the overwhelming reason for its success, is often a footnote in suffrage history. Credit for passage of the 19th Amendment is generally directed to Carrie Chapman Catt, her nemesis, and Woodrow Wilson, who opposed suffrage to the bitter end.

Alice as evidenced in her later conversations, was okay with that too.

# Epilogue

*"There will never be a new world order until women are a part of it."* Single-minded in her commitment to the equality of women, Alice Paul worked for the rest of her life for passage of the ERA and played a significant role in adding protection for women to the Civil Rights Act of 1964. After law school  she was also a founder of the World Woman's Party in 1938, which lobbied successfully for the inclusion of equality provisions in the United Nations Charter and in the 1948 Universal Declaration of Human Rights. Her legacy lives on in the continued presence of the National Women's Party, quartered in the Belmont/ Paul House in Washington, DC WWW.Nationalwomensparty.org

# Appendix 1

### A Belated Shout Out to Some of all Those Who Also Served

For Alice Paul, inspiration bounced back. She took pride in her fellow suffragists and their determination was a direct reflection of her inspired leadership. In all, about 500 women were arrested in DC and Boston demonstrations, but for a variety of reasons only 168 were actually jailed. Doris Stevens lists each woman's name in *Jailed,* her graphic review of the actions which caused the incarceration of the suffragists.

Mary Nolan, at age 73, was equally manhandled. "A man sprang at me and caught me by the shoulder. I remember saying, "I'll come with you; don't drag me; I have a lame foot." But I was jerked down the steps and into the dark."[112]

Doris Stevens' comprehensive history of the suffragist movement *Jailed for Freedom* offers an invaluable primary resource into the plodding progress of the movement,

---

[112] Stevens, ed O'Hare, p. 123

(19131919). Her clandestine lover and later husband, lawyer Dudley Field Malone, was largely responsible for the exposure of the brutality inflicted on the women that resulted in their release.

Rose Winslow came from Poland to America as an infant because her parents wanted her to become a citizen of a "free country." At age eleven she was put to work in a fourteen- hour shift weaving hosiery in a Pennsylvania Mill. This experience gave her tuberculosis and a firm resolve to aid women workers by allowing them to vote. While confined together to the prison's hospital ward, Rose and Alice agreed that the publicity of a hunger strike was their most powerful weapon. It worked. The administration was reluctantly forced to acknowledge the suffragists' case.

Maud Younger was not force fed; she fed others. She was dubbed "The Millionaire Waitress" since she was both. After a stint in a New York City settlement house, the San Francisco socialite took a job as a waitress and recognizing the urgency of the vote for working women, joined the National Women's Party in 1916. While Alice Paul fasted, Maud Younger toured the country on the Prison Special, highlighting the abuse of women prisoners.

Harriot *Stanton* Blatch was as her name implies, the daughter of famed suffragist, Elizabeth Cady Stanton. She was zealous in carrying out her mother's mission. Upon returning to America from England and her association with the Pankhursts, she revitalized the sagging suffragists. Ultimately after years of parades and protests, Harriot's efforts were rewarded with the passage of the New York State Constitutional Amendment in 1917 which finally granted women the right to vote.

Some famous women were suffragist supporters. Among them were Helen Keller, Jeanette Rankin, Dorothy Day, and Katherine Hepburn. Many more, unsung heroines contributed their time and talents, picketing and protesting, facing hostile crowds and prison. Brave women served, such as Mable Vernon, Vida Milholland, Inez' sister, and mother and daughter, Lucy Branham who shared a name and a passion.

Black Women Leaders were confronted with a barrage of problems, among which was the rights of all women to vote. White suffragists, despite their rhetoric advocating equality, rarely included black women in their organizations; discrimination was largely the norm in their times. Additionally, the suffragist leaders were so determined to win their cause, they would fear alienating their biased members and losing membership and political clout.

Black women simply formed their own groups, and in 1896, they founded the National Association of Colored Women. They could build on their legacy of exceptional women who had boldly confronted the entrenched walls of the small-minded traditions of their times.

Literally standing tall in words and stature, over six foot, Sojourner Truth (1797-1883) was the most eloquent of the earliest Black Suffragists. As a New Yorker, having been sold first at age nine for $100. and a flock of sheep, she was finally freed when the New York Anti-Slavery law was passed in 1827. So ahead of her times, so brave, she changed her given name to become Sojourner Truth and commenced her lifelong mission to gain equality for all women black and white.

Along the way, her journey took her to Akron, Ohio where she delivered her most famous speech, "Ain't I a Woman? Where she pointed out the contrast between the social acceptance of white women as opposed to black women. In yet another speech, she was interrupted and accused of being a man. Flaunting all convention, Sojourner tore open her shirt to display her breasts; no doubt she was a woman.

221

Ever prescient, she anticipated the eventuality of the Abolitionist movement, where black men would be granted the vote, and black women would be denied, having had words with the respected Frederick Douglas. Sojourner commented on the issue in 1867, when female suffrage was still very much being debated: "I feel that I have the right to have just as much as a man. There is a great stir about colored men getting their rights, but not a word about the colored women; and if colored men get their rights, and colored women not theirs, the colored men will be masters over the women, and it will be just as bad as it was before."

Ida B. Wells-Barnett, (1862-1931) had even more on her mind than votes for women. In 1884, she was peacefully riding in a train car reserved for white women, when three burly train workers approached and dragged her from the car.

She'd paid her money for a ticket and was furious at her treatment, so she sued and won. A small victory, though, when the verdict was overthrown by the Tennessee Supreme Court. One wonders if she got her ticket money back.

But Ida was not discouraged. She was a journalist as well as an educator. One of her dear friends was lynched and her newspaper, the *Memphis Free Speech*, published extensive information on the injustice of white mob violence. So the white mob turned on her instead, burned down her press and drove her from Memphis. She escaped to Chicago and championed her causes, especially the crime of black lynching. Ever bold in the face of discrimination, she famously marched in the white section of the Alice Paul's March, 1913 parade.

Mary Church Terrell (1863-1954) majored in Classics at Oberlin College, where she edited *The Oberlin Review*, and became one of the first African-American women to attend the institution, returning again to earn her master's degree in 1888. After receiving her degrees, she embarked upon a distinguished career as an activist and journalist. Along with

Ida B. Wells-Barnett becoming one of the founding members of the National Association for the Advancement of Colored People (NAACP).

Although Mary Church Terrell was a member of the National American Woman Suffrage Association, it was to Alice Paul's Congressional Union she turned to join the suffragist's picket line demonstrating at the White House.

Though these women were prominent African-American suffragists, the movement for women's votes was fought by many lesser known heroines. Daisy Lampkin spoke for suffrage on street corners in Pittsburg, and served faithfully on the Colored Voters' Division of the Republican National Committee. Francis Ellen Watkins Harper a suffragist sympathizer, also in 1858, refused to ride in the "colored section" of a segregated trolley car, 100 years before Rosa Parks did likewise. Mary Ann Shad Cary advocated for suffrage and many black issues. Cary as a member of the NASWA was a colleague of Susan B. Anthony and Elizabeth Cady Stanton. She graduated at age 60 from Howard University as the second African-American Lawyer in history.

Black suffragists, though often unfairly treated, maintained their integrity and recognized themselves as beneficiaries of the movement for women's equality. Unfortunately, it was the Northern black women who voted; until the 1960's southern states managed to erect barriers to prevent all black, male and female enfranchisement. Unfortunately, to this day, in some southern places, the fight for a black citizen's right to vote persists.

There were fair-minded men also supported votes for women. Dudley Field Malone and his fellow lawyer, Matthew O'Brien worked feverously to free the Silent Sentinels from prison. Theodore Roosevelt encouraged Republicans to vote for the Anthony Amendment. New Yorker Colonel William Boyce Thompson put his money into the mix. He contributed ten thousand dollars to the suffrage campaign, "one hundred dollars for each of the pickets who went to prison because she stood at the gates of the White House, asking for the passage of the suffrage measure."[113]

Though common sense justice would ultimately have granted women their rights, these and others unnamed here, brought closure to the national disgrace sooner rather than later.

# Appendix II
## Education for Women: A Painful Birth

Education for women finally and inevitably emerged in the 1800's. Dr. Edward Clarke stated "A woman's body could only handle a limited number of developmental tasks at one time-that girls who spent too much energy developing their minds during puberty would end up with undeveloped or diseased reproductive systems.[114]

But others thought otherwise.

Common Schools began in earnest in 1830's New England. Horace Mann, Secretary of Education, successfully argued that all children had a right to be educated.

Finishing School = Private Girls' schools for the very wealthy only. They were designed to prepare students to be suitable wives.

Academy: Secondary schools began to flourish in the early 1800s, but Young Ladies Academies did not require students to stay for a set period of time and the curriculum varied with location. In 1847 the Sisters of Charity of New

---

[113] Ibid p.138
[114] Cott, Nancy F. (1987) The Grounding of Modern Feminism, Yale University Press, pp. 51-82

York founded the Academy of Mt. St. Vincent, the first institution to offer higher learning for women in New York.

Female Seminary:  Founded c. 1815. Schools which were more serious than Academies. The goal of these schools was to provide an education for women that was equal to men's education. Catherine Beecher founded the Hartford Female Seminary and hired eight teachers who would focus on such topics as philosophy, chemistry, mathematics and Latin

Coeducation: The abolitionists who founded Oberlin College in 1833, went wild with the unthinkable. From the founding, they accepted both women and men, black and white. This was despite the worries about women being educated alongside men when it was common knowledge that women would suffer nervous breakdowns if they were to compete in a man's world.

It seemed that girls just wanted to have smarts and many who could, began to attend college. Mount Holyoke College (1836) and Vassar, (1861) were educating females, though one of the prevailing rumors hinted that a learned woman would make an unfit mother and/or be unable to bear children. The egalitarian Quaker founders of Swarthmore (1864) even encouraged both women and men to enroll, but not to mingle.

Westward, attitudes were somewhat more enlightened, though in Ohio, at Oberlin, (1833) women were not allowed to participate in "men's courses."  Grinnell, (1846) in Iowa, also took the lead and graduated its first woman in 1865, when Joanna Harris Haines respectfully received a specific "diploma" purposely made equal to the definitely male tainted "bachelor's degree." University of Iowa, in 1855, was the first co-ed state university to admit women, but just because they were admitted into a coeducation college didn't mean that they were equals.

In the east, Coordinate Colleges were founded. Radcliffe College (1894) was a "Harvard Annex," but it took until 1963, 69 years later, till women were able to receive a Harvard degree.

# Videos

*The Suffragette* kultur.com

*Suffragette* Universal Studios.com

*Iron Jawed Angels* HBO Films

Ken Burns and Paul Barnes: Elizabeth Cady Stanton & Susan B. Anthony *Not for Ourselves Alone* Dolly Parton 27 The Most Perfect
Album *Nineteenth Amendment*

YouTube "The Vinegar Tasters"

## Historic Sites to Visit Alice

Paul Institute "Paulsville" Mt. Laurel, N.J. Alicepaul.org

Occoquan Workhouse, Lorton, VA Workhousearts.org

Belmont/Paul House, Washington, DC

# BIBLIOGRAPY

## Primary Sources

Alice Paul Papers
Radcliffe.harvard.edu/Schlesingerlibrary/collection/
Alice-Paul

Dorr, Rheta Childe. Susan B. Anthony: *The Woman Who Changed the Mind of a Nation*. New York, NY: Frederick A. Stokes, 1928.

Irwin, Inez Haynes. *The Story of Alice Paul and the National Woman's Party*. Edgewater. FL.: Denlinger's Publishers, 1977

Pankhurst, Emmeline. *My Own Story.*London: Eveleigh Nash, 1914.

Stevens, Doris. *Jailed for Freedom*. Troutdale, OR: New Sage Press, 1995.

Stanton, Elizabeth Cady; Susan B. Anthony; and Matilda Joslyn Gage. *History of Woman Suffrage. Vol.1, 1848-1861*. Rochester, NY, London, Paris: Source: Book Press, 1899.

## Secondary Sources

Cahill, Bernadette. *Alice Paul, the National Woman's Party and the Vote, The first Civil Rights Struggle of the 20th Century*. Jefferson, NC: MacFarland & Company, Inc., Publishers, 2015.

Lumsden, Linda J. Inez, *The Life and Times of Inez Milholland*. Bloomington, IN: Indiana University Press.

Lunardini, Christine. *From Equal Suffrage to Equal Rights, Alice Paul and the National Woman's Party, 1910-1928*. Lincoln, NE: toExcel Press, 1986.

Neumann, Johanna. *Gilded Suffragists*. New York, NY:Washington Mews Books, 2017

Walton, Mary. *A Woman's Crusade: Alice Paul and the Battle for the Ballot*. New York: Palgrave Macmillan, 2010.

Yellin, Carol Lynn, and Janann Sherman. *The Perfect 36 Tennessee Delivers Woman Suffrage*. Oak Ridge, TN: Iris Press, 1998.

Zahniser, J.D, & Fry, Amelia R. *Alice Paul, Claiming Power*. Oxford, UK: Oxford University Press, 2014.

# Are You a Suffragist Descendent?

Over 500 women were arrested during the campaign for women's right to vote. Doris Stevens' first-hand account, *Jailed for Freedom*, lists the names, cities and brief bios of those 168 brave women who were unjustly imprisoned for their right to vote. Listed below are those suffragists who resisted. They come from all over the country and range in age from Mary Nolan's 73 years to 19 year-old Matilda Young.

With today's technology it is easily possible to identify our ancestors and take pride in their selfless service, especially when the 100th Anniversary of the Anthony Amendment is celebrated in 2020.

Are you related to one of these amazing women? Find her on line in an ancestry search for family trees. Contact patriciacuff.com for more information on each woman listed.

Minnie D.Abbott, Atlantic City, N.J

Pauline Adams,  Norfolk, VA

Edith Ainge, Jamestown, NY

Harriet Andrews, Kansas City, MO

Annie Arniel, Wilmington, DE

Berthe Arnold, Colorado Springs, CO

Virginia Arnold, NC

W. D. Ascough, Detroit, MI

Amy Scott Baker, Washington,DC

Mrs. Charles W. Barnes. IN

Naomi Barrett, Wilmington, DE

Mrs. W.J. Bartlett, Putnam, CT

Mrs. M. T.  Bennett, Hartford, ,CT

Hilda Blumberg, New York, NY

Kate Boeckh, Washington, DC

Catherine Boyle, Newcastle, DE

Lucy G. Branham, Baltimore, MD

Lucy G. Branham (Mother) Baltimore,

Mrs. John Winters Brannan, New York, NY

Jennie Bronenberg, Philadelphia, PA

Mrs. Mary E. Brown, Wilmington, DE

Louise Bryant, New York, NY

Lucy Burns, Brooklyn, NY

Mrs. Henry Butterworth, New York, NY

Mrs. Lucille E.A. Calme, Princeton, IA

Eleanor Calnan, Metheun, MA

Mrs. Palys I. Chevrier, New York, NY

Josephine Collins, Framingham, MA

Sarah Tarlet, on Colvin, St. Paul, MN

Betty Connolly, West Newton, MA

Alice M. Cosu, New Orleans, LA

Cora Crawford, Philadelphia, PA

Gertrude Crocker, Washington, DC

Ruth Crocker, Washington, DC

Mrs. L.J.C. Daniels, Grafton, VT

Dorothy Day, New York, NY

Edna Dixon, Washington, DC

Lavinia Dock, Fayetteville, PA

Mary Carroll Dowell, Philadelphia, PA

Mary Dubrow, Passaic, NJ

Mary C. Dowell, Philadelphia, PA

Julia Emory, Baltimore, MD

Mrs. Edmund C. Evans, Ardmore, PA

Lucy Ewing, Chicago, IL

Estella Eylward, New Orleans, LA

Mary Gertrude Fendall, Baltimore, MD

Ella Findeisen. Lawrence, MA

Fisher, Washington, DC

Rose Gratz Fishstein, Philadelphia, PA

Rose Fishstein,, Philadelphia, PA

Catherine M. Flanagan, Hartford, CT

Martha Foley, Dorchester, MA

Mrs. T.W. Forbes, Baltimore, MD

Hazel Hunsins, Billings, MT

Martha Foley, Dorchester, MA

Mrs. T.W. Forbes, Baltimore, MD

Janet Fotheringham, Buffalo, NY

Margaret Fotheringham, Buffalo, NY

Francis Fowler, Brookline, MA

Mrs. Matilda H. Gardiner, Wash. DC

Anna Ginsberg, New York, NY

Reba Gomrorov, Philadelphia, PA

Alice Gram, Portland, OR

Betty Gram, Portland, OR

Mrs. Francis Green, New York, NY

Gladys Greiner, Baltimore, MD

Mrs. J. Irving Gross, Boston, MA

Anna Gwinter, New York, NY

Elizabeth Hamilton, New York, NY

Ernestine Hara, New York, NY

Rebecca Harrison, Joplin, MO

Mrs. H.G. Havemeyer, New York, NY

Mrs. Jessica Henderson, Boston, MA

Minnie Hennesey, Hartford, CT.

Anne Herkimer, Baltimore, MD Katherine

Elsie Hill, Norwalk, CT.

Mrs. George Hill, Boston, MA

Mrs. Florence B. Hilles, Newcastle, DE

Mrs. J.A.H. Hopkins, Morristown, NJ

Mrs. I.H., Hornbby, New York, NY

Elizabeth, Hoff, Des Moines, IA

Louise Parker Mayo, Framingham, MA

Julia Hurlbut, Morristown, NJ

Mary Ingram, Philadelphia, PA

Mrs. Mark Jackson, Baltimore, MD

Paula Jacobi, New York, NY

Maud Jamison, Norfolk, VA

Peggy Baird Johns, New York, NY

Willie Grace Johnson, Shreveport, LA

Amy Juengling, Buffalo, NY

Elizabeth Green Kalb, Houston, TX

Rhoda Kellogg, Minneapolis, MN

Mrs. Frederick W. Kendall, Hamburg, NY

Marie Ernst Kennedy, Philadelphia, PA

Margaret Wood Kessler, Denver, CO

Alice Kimball, New York City

Beatrice Kinkead, Monclair, NJ

Ruby E. Koenig, Hartford,

Hattie Kruger, Buffalo, NY

Dr. Anna Kuhn, Baltimore, MD

Mrs. Lawrence Lewis, Philadelphia, PA

Katherine Lincoln, New York City

Dr. Sarah H. Lockrey, Philadelphia, PA

Elizabeth McShane, Philadelphia, PA

Annie J. Magee, Wilmington, DE

Effie B. Main, Topeka, KS

Maud Malone, New York, NY

Anne Martin, Reno, NV

Louise Parker Mayo, Framingham, MA

Vida Milholland, New York, NY

Nell Mercer, Norfolk, VA

Vida Milholland, New York, NY

. Bertha Moller, Minneapolis, MN

Martha W. Moore, Philadelphia, PA

Mrs. Agnes H. Morey, Brookline, MA

Katherine Morey, Brookline, MA

Mildred Morris, Denver, CO

Phoebe C. Munnecke, Detroit, Mich.

Gertrude Murphy, Minneapolis, Minn.

Mary A. Nolan, Jacksonville, FL

Mrs. Margaret Oakis, Idaho

Alice Paul, Moorestown, NJ

Berry Pottier, Boston, MA

Edna M. Purtelle, Hartford, CT

Mrs. R.B. Quay, Salt Lake City, Utah

Mrs. Betsy Reyneau, Detroit, MI

Mrs. John Rogers, Jr. New York, NY

Marguerite Rossetti, Baltimore, MD

Elsie T. Russian, Detroit, MI

Nina Samarodin, Kiev, Russia

Phoebe P. Scott, Morristown, NJ

Ruth Scott, Bridgeport, CT

Belle Sheinberg, New York, NY

Lucille Shields, Amarillo, TX

Martha R. Shoemaker, Philadelphia, PA

Mary Short, Minnapolis, Minn.

Lois Warren Shaw, Manchester, NH

Ruth Small, Boston, MA

Dr.Caroline E. Spenceer, Colorado Spr. CO

Kate Stafford, Oklahoma City, OK

Doris Stevens, Omaha, NE

Elizabeth Stuyvesant, New York, NY

Elsie Unterman, Chicago, IL

Mabel Vernon, Wilmington, DE

Elsie Vervane, Bridgeport, CT

Iris Calderhead, Marysville, KS

Mrs. Robert Walker, Baltimore. MD

Bertha Wallerstein, New York, NY     Bertha

Walmsley, Kansas City, MO

Mrs. William Upton Watson, Chicago, IL

Mrs. C. Weaver, Bridgeport, CT

Eva Weaver, Daughter, Bridgeport, CT

Helena Hill Weed, Norwalk, CT

Cora A. Week, New York, NY

Camilla Whitcomb, Worcester, MA

Sue White, Jackson, TN

Margaret Fay Whittemore, Detroit, MI

Mrs. Harvey W. Wiley, Washington, DC

Rose Winslow, New York, NY

Mary Winsor, Haverford, PA

Ellen Winsor, Haverford, PA

Kate Winston, Chevy Chase, MD

Clara Wold, Portland, OR

Joy Young, New York, NY

Matilda Young, Washington, DC

# Some Questions for Book Club Discussions

- ➢ The place of money in politics, good or bad? Who are more effective as legislative advocates, big donors or energized voters?
- ➢ Why and how do women enter politics? Is 2018 an historic, watershed year? Will men always predominate in politics?
- ➢ How did racial bias factor into the suffrage movement and the passage of the Anthony Amendment?
- ➢ Which aggression works best, passive or aggressive? Whose methods were more successful, Alice Paul or Carrie Chapman Catt? Could and should they have worked together?
- ➢ Alice Paul largely authored the Equal Rights Amendment; Carrie Chapman Catt folded NASWA into the League of Women Voters. Are these equal legacies?
- ➢ How is women's suffrage treated in the history texts?
- ➢ Is virtue its own reward? Look for modest Alice in the history texts.
- ➢ Who determines the content of history texts? Are history texts aimed at a specific audience?

# Index

241

Quakers (Friends) 16, 19, 20, 21, 23, 39, 44, 49, 80, 108, 151, 152

Rankin, Jeanette, 152, 153, 193, 219

Ratification: Nineteenth Amendment, 82, 188, 100, 210-212,

Republican, 100, 107, 111, 113, 137, 192-194, 198, 200, 204, 209, 212, 222

Republican Party, 107, 137

Rhode Island, 111, 114, 121, 124

Rogers, Elizabeth Selden, 92, 100, 162, 230

Roosevelt, Theodore, 120, 222

Russia, 155, 156, 160, 230

Russian Banner, 155, 156, 160

Senate 74, 83, 99, 100, 102, 109, 154, 165, 194, -196, 202, 203, 206, 207, 209, 211, 212Y

Seneca Falls Convention, 17, 75,

Settlement Houses, 35, 38, 212

Shafroth-Palmer Amendment, 107, 109

Shaw, Anna Howard, 65, 67, 74, 78, 96, 101-106, 108. 112, 130, 160, 184, 192

Silent Sentinels, (See Pickets)

Stanton, Elizabeth Cady, 17, 75, 80, 151, 225,

Stevens, Doris, 51, 137, 143, 146, 150, 162, 163, 166, 176, 185, 193, 197, 201, 202, 218, 228, 231

# Notes

Made in the USA
Middletown, DE
24 December 2019